What Year am I?

A Math Warm-up a Day

Hope Martin

Hope's Books   P.O. Box 1693   Skokie, Ilinois

User's Guide
to
Hope's Books

Our philosophy at Hope's Books is to provide stimulating, enriching, and interactive materials for teachers to use in their classrooms. All materials have been designed with this basic policy in mind:

Hope's Books grants individual purchasers of this book the right to make sufficient copies of reproducible pages for all students of a single teacher. This permission is limited to a single teacher and does not apply to entire schools or school systems, so institutions purchasing the book should pass the permission on to a single teacher. Student pages may be considered blackline masters and may be converted to overhead transparencies for use in a single teacher's classroom. Copying of this book or its parts for resale is prohibited and in violation of United States Copyright Laws.

Any questions about this policy or requests to purchase further reproduction rights should be addressed to:

Permissions Editor
Hope's Books
P.O. Box 1693
Skokie, IL. 60076-1693

10   9   8   7   6   5   4   3   2   1

ISBN 0-9659993-0-0

Hope's Books
P.O. Box 1693
Skokie, IL 60076-1693

To the Teacher

Don't you find that your students just love working out puzzles? It seems that we can convince them to do *just about anything* if we present it in the form of a game or poser. The activities presented in *What Year am I?* do just that – they present important mathematical concepts and skills in the form of puzzles! But they do even more. They make important connections for students between math and other areas of the curriculum. If you convert each date into transparencies and place them on the overhead, your students will be learning new (or reinforcing old) math skills and concepts while they use deductive reasoning skills to solve interesting puzzles related to historical events.

The National Council of Mathematics *Curriculum and Evaluation Standards for School Mathematics* encourages us to use problem situations as the context for mathematics, include problems that arise from "real world" situations, encourage the belief that mathematics is reasoning (and not just the memorization of rules and procedures), and give our students the opportunity to see that mathematics is, indeed, *a sense-making experience.*

The puzzles contained in *What Year am I?* inspire students to use their math skills and reasoning abilities. They solve problems that make connections between mathematics and their real world. When students solve a puzzle, they learn the year that a particular historical event took place — these range from the invention of the ice-cream cone to the birth date of Dr. Sally Kirsten Ride, the first woman in space.

Because the mathematical clues are so dependent on the particular date, no attempt has been made to sequence math concepts or skills. It is assumed that skills will be learned within the context of the problems. The daily puzzles should take just a few minutes for students to complete but time should be devoted for students to "share their thinking." Perhaps students can come up to the overhead and explain how they solved the problem. Follow-up questions should always be, "Did anyone solve it a different way?" or "Did anyone get a different answer?"

By working the puzzles in *What Year am I?* your students will be given the opportunity to explore many math skills and concepts. Some are:

- computation with whole numbers
- introductory fraction concepts
- place value
- money values
- calendar facts
- introduction to prime numbers
- names of polygons
- perimeter, area and volume
- number sequences
- introductory divisibility rules
- factors and multiples
- odds and evens
- mathematical terms and vocabulary
- measurement equivalents
- averages
- beginning algebra concepts (missing number problems)
- passage of time
- palindromes

If your students work on these puzzles daily, they will become more confident problem-solvers and learn to solve problems using their reasoning skills and the context clues provided in the puzzle. If you wish, you can assign week-end dates for homework – students can work with their parents to solve the puzzles. So . . .Why not start your math lesson by getting your students into a *mathematical frame of mind* with a math warmup a day from *What Year am I?* Have fun with your students.

Hope Martin

Glossary of Terms

area of rectangle

The product of the length and the width: $A = l \cdot w$

area of triangle

Half the product of the base and the height:
$A = \frac{1}{2}(b \cdot h)$

counting numbers

1, 2, 3, 4, 5, . . .

decagon

A polygon with ten sides

difference

The solution to a subtraction problem

divisibility rules   **A number is divisible by:**

2: if it is even
3: if the sum of the digits is divisible by 3
4: if the number is even and the last two digits are divisible by 4
5: if the last digit is a 5 or a 0
6: if the number is divisible by both 2 and 3
10: if the number ends in a 0

even numbers

0, 2, 4, 6, 8, . . .

Greatest Common Factor

The largest factor that two or more numbers have in common; e.g.   the factors of 8: 1, 2, 4, and 8
the factors of 12: 1, 2, 3, 4, 6, and 12
The Greatest Common Factor of 8 and 12 is 4.

hexagon

A polygon with six sides

Least Common Multiple

The smallest multiple that two or more numbers have in common; e.g. the multiples of 2: 2, 4, 6, 8, . . .
the multiples of 3: 3, 6, 9, 12, . . .
The Least Common Multiple of 2 and 3 is 6.

nonagon

A polygon with nine sides

octagon

A polygon with eight sides

odd numbers

1, 3, 5, 7, 9, . . .

palindrome

A number which appears the same whether it is read from left to right or right to left; e.g. 1881 is a palindrome.

pentagon	A polygon with five sides
perimeter	The sum of the lengths of the sides of a polygon
prime number	A number that has only two factors, one and itself
product	The solution to a multiplication problem
quadrilateral	A polygon with four sides
quotient	The solution to a division problem
rectangle	A quadrilateral with four right angles and opposite sides that are congruent (having the same measure)
square	A quadrilateral with four congruent sides and four right angles
sum	The solution to an addition problem
triangle	A polygon with three sides
volume	The capacity of a 3-dimensional figure: $V = l \cdot w \cdot h$

January 1st

On January 1st of this year Betsy Ross was born. She was the needleworker who designed the first flag of the United States. In what year did this happen? Solve this puzzle to find the answer.

- My units digit is equal to $25 \div 5$.
- My hundreds digit times my tens digit is 49.
- The sum of all of my digits is 20.

What year am I? ___ ___ ___ ___

Thousands Hundreds Tens Units

January 2nd

On January 2nd of this year the first junior high school was opened in the United States.Solve this puzzle to find the year it opened.

- The two-digit number formed by my tens and units digits is equal to $100 \div 10$.
- The sum of my thousands and hundreds digits is 10.
- The sum of all of my digits is 11.

What year am I? ___ ___ ___ ___

Thousands Hundreds Tens Units

January 3rd

On January 3rd of this year margarine was first patented. Solve this puzzle to find the year that "imitation butter" was first invented.

- My thousands digit is the same as my units digit.
- My hundreds digit is the same as the number of sides in an octagon.
- My tens digit is the missing number: $8 \times \square = 56$
- The sum of all of my digits is 17.

What year am I? ____ ____ ____ ____

Thousands Hundreds Tens Units

January 4th

January 4th is the birthday of Louis Braille, the man who invented a way for blind people to read and write. To discover the year Louis Braille was born, just solve this puzzle.

- My units digit is equal to $7 + 2$.
- My hundreds digit is equal to my units digit minus 1.
- My tens digit is equal to my thousands digit minus 1.
- The sum of all of my digits is 18.

What year am I? ____ ____ ____ ____

Thousands Hundreds Tens Units

January 5th

On January 5th of this year George Washington Carver, a great African-American scientist, died. Although born as a slave, he discovered many uses for peanuts, potatoes, and wood. His birthplace is a national monument. Solve this puzzle to discover the year George Washington Carver died.

- The sum of my even tens digit and odd units digit is 7; their difference is 1.
- My hundreds digit minus 1 = 8.
- The sum of all of my digits is 17.

What year am I? __ __ __ __

Thousands Hundreds Tens Units

January 6th

Joan of Arc, the French saint and national heroine, was born on January 6th. She fought against the English armies when they invaded France. Solve this puzzle to find the year Joan of Arc was believed to be born.

- The two-digit number formed by my tens and units digits is the product of 4 and 3.
- The two-digit number formed by my thousands and hundreds digit is the product of 7 and 2.
- The sum of my digits is the missing number:
   ☐ x 6 = 48.

What year am I? __ __ __ __

Thousands Hundreds Tens Units

What Year am I?

January 7th

On January 7th of this year the first bank was opened in Philadelphia, Pennsylvania. To find out what year this bank opened, just solve this puzzle.

- My even units digit multiplied by 4 equals my tens digit.
- My tens digit minus 1 equals my hundreds digit.
- My hundreds digit is the missing number in this problem: □ x 8 = 56.
- The sum of all of my digits is 18.

What year am I? ____ ____ ____ ____

Thousands Hundreds Tens Units

January 8th

On January 8th of this year Bobby Fischer won the U.S. chess championship for the first time. He was 14 years old at the time. Solve this puzzle to find the year that Bobby Fischer became champion.

- My hundreds digit times my units digit equals 72.
- My hundreds digit is one greater than my units digit.
- My tens digit is the number of sides in a pentagon.
- The sum of all of my digits is 23.

What year am I? ____ ____ ____ ____

Thousands Hundreds Tens Units

January 9th

On January 9th of this year Jean Pierre Blanchard made the first manned hot-air balloon flight in America. The balloon rose about 5800 feet and stayed up about 3/4 of an hour. Jean Pierre had one passenger, his little dog. Solve this puzzle to discover the year this happened.

- My tens digit is three times the size of my units digit; they are both odd numbers.
- My hundreds digit plus 2 is equal to my tens digit.
- My tens digit times my hundreds digit is equal to 63.

What year am I? ___ ___ ___ ___

Thousands Hundreds Tens Units

January 10th

On January 10th of this year Ethan Allen was born. He was the leader of Vermont's "Green Mountain Boys" and a hero of the Revolutionary War. Solve this problem to find the year Ethan Allen was born.

- The sum of my thousands and hundreds digits equals my units digit.
- My hundreds digit is the number of days in one week.
- The sum of all of my digits = 38 ÷ 2.

What year am I? ___ ___ ___ ___

Thousands Hundreds Tens Units

January 11th

Have you ever had rhubarb pie? On January 11th of this year England first sent rhubarb to America. To discover the year, just solve this puzzle.

- My thousands digit and units digit are the same number: the first counting number.
- My tens digit plus 1 equals my hundreds digit.
- The product of my hundreds and tens digit is 42.

What year am I? ___ ___ ___ ___

Thousands Hundreds Tens Units

January 12th

On January 12th of this year the first X-ray was made. Have you ever had an X-ray taken? To find out when the first X-ray was made, just solve this puzzle.

- The product of my odd tens digit and even units digit is 54.
- My units digit is the same as the number of sides in a hexagon.
- $72 \div 9$ is equal to my hundreds digit.
- The sum of all of my digits is 24.

What year am I? ___ ___ ___ ___

Thousands Hundreds Tens Units

January 13th

On January 13th of this year Stephen Foster, a great American musician, died. This day has been named "Stephen Foster Memorial Day" in his honor. Solve this puzzle to find out the year of Mr. Foster's death.

- The two digit number formed by my tens and units digit is the quotient of this problem: $832 \div 13 =$
- My hundreds digit is the same as the number of sides in an octagon.
- The sum of all of my digits is 19.

What year am I? __ __ __ __

Thousands   Hundreds   Tens   Units

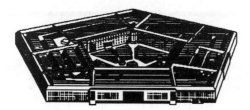

January 14th

On January 14th of this year, the Pentagon building was finished. Do you know who uses the Pentagon? To find out when the Pentagon was built, just solve this puzzle.

- My tens digit minus 1 is equal to my units digit.
- The product of my units and tens digits is 12.
- My hundreds digit is three times bigger than my units digit.
- The sum of all of my digits is the difference between 562 and 545.

What year am I? __ __ __ __

Thousands   Hundreds   Tens   Units

Dr. Martin Luther King, Jr.

January 15th

On January 15th Dr. Martin Luther King, Jr. was born in Atlanta, Georgia. He was a minister, a civil rights leader, and a winner of the Nobel Peace Prize. To find out when this great American was born, just solve this puzzle.

- The two-digit number formed by my tens and units digits is the quotient of this problem: $174 \div 6 =$
- The two-digit number formed by my thousands and hundreds digits is ten less than the quotient above.
- The sum of all of my digits is equal to 7×3.

What year am I? ___ ___ ___ ___

Thousands Hundreds Tens Units

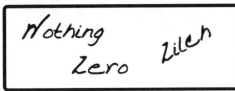

Nothing
Zero   Zilch

January 16th

January 16th was named by a newspaper man, Harold Coffin, as "Nothing Day" so that Americans could have at least one day a year when they didn't have to celebrate anything or honor anyone! To find out the first year of "non celebration," solve this puzzle.

- The sum of my thousands and hundreds digits is equal to the sum of my tens and units digits.
- The product of my thousands and hundreds digits is 9; the product of my tens and units digits is 21.
- My units digit is 1/3 my hundreds digit.

What year am I? ___ ___ ___ ___

Thousands Hundreds Tens Units

What Year am I?

January 17th

Benjamin Franklin was born in Boston, Massachusetts, on January 17th. He was the oldest signer of the Declaration of Independence and the Constitution, as well as a scientist, a printer, a publisher, and a philosopher. To learn the year of his birth, just solve this puzzle.

- My hundreds digit minus my thousands digit is equal to my units digit.
- My tens digit is one less than my thousands digit.
- My units digit is the same as the number of sides on a hexagon.
- The sum of my digits is the product of 7 and 2.

What year am I? __ __ __ __

Thousands Hundreds Tens Units

January 18th

January 18th is "Pooh Day" to celebrate the birthday of A.A. Milne. Milne, the English author, wrote *Winnie the Pooh* and *The House at Pooh Corner*. To learn when A.A. Milne was born, solve this puzzle.

- My hundreds and tens digits could be the sides of a square (remember, all sides must be the same size). The perimeter of this square would be 32.
- My units digit is the first even number.
- The sum of my digits is one more than one dozen.

What year am I? __ __ __ __

Thousands Hundreds Tens Units

What Year am I?

January 19th

On January 19th of this year the idea for putting food into tin cans was patented. Do you know what a patent is? Solve this problem to find the year of this invention.

- My tens and unit digits form a number that is 1/4 of 100.
- My hundreds digit is the same as the average of these numbers: 14, 4, and 6.
- The sum of my digits is equal to my hundreds digit times 2.

What year am I? __ __ __ __

Thousands Hundreds Tens Units

January 20th

On January 20th of this year the first basketball game was played in the U.S. James Naismith, a YMCA instructor, invented the game so children would have something to do indoors when it was raining or snowing outside. Solve this problem to discover the year.

- My tens digit is one larger than my hundreds digit.
- The product of my tens and hundreds digits is 72.
- My units digit is the Greatest Common Factor of 4 and 6.

What year am I? __ __ __ __

Thousands Hundreds Tens Units

What Year am I?

January 21st

January 21st of this year was the first time people needed a driver's license to drive a car. To find out the year that this law was passed, solve this puzzle.

- My units digit is the same as the digit in the hundreds place of this number: 23,715.
- My tens digit is four less than my units digit.
- My hundreds digit is three times the size of my tens digit.
- The sum of all of my digits is equal to 20.

What year am I? ___ ___ ___ ___
Thousands Hundreds Tens Units

January 22nd

On January 22nd Joseph Wambaugh celebrates his birthday. Mr. Wambaugh was a police officer and is now an author. He writes adult murder mysteries. To discover the year he was born, just solve this puzzle.

- My tens digit times itself is equal to my hundreds digit; both are odd numbers.
- My units digit is the average of these numbers: 10, 5, and 6.
- The sum of all of my digits is the missing number in this problem: □ x 4 = 80.

What year am I? ___ ___ ___ ___
Thousands Hundreds Tens Units

January 23rd

On January 23rd of this year John Hancock was born. He was the first person to sign the Declaration of Independence. Solve this problem to find the year John was born.

- The two-digit number formed by my tens and units digit is the difference between 295 and 258.
- My hundreds digit is the same as my units digit.
- The sum of all of my digits is 18.

What year am I? __ __ __ __

Thousands   Hundreds   Tens   Units

January 24th

On January 24th of this year John Sutter discovered gold in California. Find out the year of the "Gold Rush" by solving this puzzle..

- My hundreds and units digits are the same; an octagon has this number of sides.
- My tens digit is 1/2 of my units digit.
- 756 ÷ 36 equals the sum of all of my digits.

What year am I? __ __ __ __

Thousands   Hundreds   Tens   Units

What Year am I?

January 25th

On January 25th of this year the first American clown was born. His name was Dan Rice. To find the year Dan was born, solve this puzzle.

- My tens digit is the only even prime number.
- My units digit is one greater than my tens digit.
- The factors of my hundreds digit are 1, 2, 4, and itself.

What year am I? ___ ___ ___ ___

Thousands Hundreds Tens Units

January 26th

On January 26th of this year Michigan became the twenty-sixth state of the United States. To find the year, solve this puzzle.

- The product of my tens and units digits is 21.
- My units digit minus 4 is equal to my tens digit.
- My hundreds digit minus my thousands digit is equal to my units digit.

What year am I? ___ ___ ___ ___

Thousands Hundreds Tens Units

What Year am I?

 # January 27th

On January 27th of this year Lewis Carroll was born. Have you read *Alice in Wonderland*? To find the year Lewis Carroll was born, solve this puzzle.

- My tens digit is the same as the area of this diagram:

- My hundreds digit is the same as its perimeter.
- My units digit is 1/4 of my hundreds digit.
- The sum of all of my digits is 14.

What year am I? ___ ___ ___ ___

Thousands Hundreds Tens Units

January 28th

On January 28th of this year the first telephone switchboard was used. Do you know what a switchboard is? To find the year of this invention, solve this puzzle.

- The Least Common Multiple of my tens and units digits is 56.
- My tens digit is only one less than my units digit.
- My hundreds digit is the Greatest Common Factor of 16 and 24.
- The sum of all of my digits is 24.

What year am I? ___ ___ ___ ___

Thousands Hundreds Tens Units

         What Year am I?

January 29th

On January 29th of this year a machine that rolled ice cream cones was patented. To find out the year of this "delicious" invention, solve this problem.

- The two-digit number formed by my tens and units digits is the perimeter of this figure:

- The two-digit number formed by thousands and hundreds digits is the answer to: $399 \div 21 =$

What year am I? __ __ __ __
Thousands Hundreds Tens Units

January 30th

On January 30th of this year the first telecast of *The Lone Ranger* was heard on the radio. Do you know the name of the Lone Ranger's horse? To find out the date of this radio show, solve this puzzle.

- My hundreds digit is three times the size of my tens digit.
- My tens digit and my units digit are the same.
- All of my digits are odd numbers.

What year am I? __ __ __ __
Thousands Hundreds Tens Units

January 31st

January 31st was the birthday of the first African-American to play major league baseball. His name was Jackie Robinson and he played for the Brooklyn Dodgers. To learn the year he was born, solve this puzzle.

- My thousands digit and my tens digit are the same.
- My product of my hundreds digit and my units digit is 81.
- The sum of all of my digits is 1/5 of 100.

What year am I? ___ ___ ___ ___

Thousands   Hundreds   Tens   Units

What Year am I?

February 1st

February 1st is the birthday of Clark Gable, the Hollywood movie star who starred as Rhett Butler in *Gone With the Wind.* Solve this puzzle to find the year he was born.

- My thousands and units digits are the same number.
- My hundreds digit is the missing number in this sequence: 1, 1, 1, 3, 5, __, 17. . .
- The sum of all of my digits is only 11.

What year am I? ___ ___ ___ ___
Thousands Hundreds Tens Units

February 2nd

On February 2nd of this year the first five charter members of the brand-new Baseball Hall of Fame were named. These players were Ty Cobb, Babe Ruth, Honus Wagner, Christy Mathewson, and Walter Johnson. Solve this puzzle to find the year this Hall of Fame opened.

- The two-digit number formed by my tens and units digits is the missing dividend: _____ ÷ 4 = 9.
- The sum of my thousands and hundreds digits is 10.
- The sum of all of my digits is the perimeter of this polygon:

What year am I? ___ ___ ___ ___
Thousands Hundreds Tens Units

February 3rd

February 3rd is called "The Day the Music Died" because it is the date the plane carrying rock and roll greats Buddy Holly (Charles Hardin), The Big Bopper (J.P. Richardson), and Richie Valens crashed. Solve this puzzle to find the year.

- The two-digit number formed by my tens and units digits is the product of 14 and 4.
- My hundreds digit is one more than the number of sides in an octagon.
- The sum of all of my digits is the change you would get from one dollar if you spent 79¢.

What year am I? ___ ___ ___ ___

Thousands Hundreds Tens Units

February 4th

February 4th is the anniversary of the Apache Wars started by Apache Chief Cochise and continued by Geronimo. To find the year this war started, just solve this puzzle.

- My thousands and units digit are the same.
- My hundreds digit is equal to the number of quarts in two gallons.
- My tens digit is the same as the number of sides in a hexagon.
- The sum of all of my digits is the missing factor: ___ x 3 = 48.

What year am I? ___ ___ ___ ___

Thousands Hundreds Tens Units

February 5th

February 5th is called "Weatherman's Day" because it is the birthday of one of America's first weathermen, John Jeffries. Solve this puzzle to discover the year John Jeffries was born.

- My tens and units digits are the same; each is the number of sides that are in a quadrilateral.
- My hundreds digit is the average of these numbers: 8, 3, 9, 10, and 5.
- The sum of all of my digits is 16.

What year am I? __ __ __ __

Thousands Hundreds Tens Units

February 6th

February 6th is the birthday of Babe Ruth, one of baseball's greatest heroes. He hit 714 homeruns and played in 10 World Series. To find the year the Babe was born, just solve this puzzle.

- My units digit is the same as the number of sides in a pentagon.
- My hundreds digit is one less than my tens digit; their sum is 17 and their product is 72.
- The sum of all of my digits is 7 more than the number of ounces in a pound.

What year am I? __ __ __ __

Thousands Hundreds Tens Units

February 7th

On February 7th of this year ballet was first introduced to the U.S. The ballet was called *The Deserter* and was performed in New York City. To find the year this happened, just solve this puzzle.

- The sum of my thousands and hundreds digits is equal to the sum of my tens and units digits.
- My tens digit is 1/4 of my hundreds digit.
- My hundreds digit is the missing number in this problem: ☐ x 7 = 56.
- The sum of all of my digits is 18.

What year am I? __ __ __ __

Thousands Hundreds Tens Units

February 8th

February 8th is the birthday of the Boy Scouts of America. It was founded by William Boyce in Washington, D.C. Solve this puzzle to find the year that the Boy Scouts got started.

- My thousands, hundreds, and tens digits form a palindrome whose sum is 11.
- The two-digit number formed by my tens and units digits is the same as the number of sides in a decagon.
- My hundreds digit is the largest single-digit number.

What year am I? __ __ __ __

Thousands Hundreds Tens Units

What Year am I?

February 9th

February 9th of this year is the birthday of the 9th president of the U.S., William Henry Harrison. His term of office – 32 days – is the shortest in our history. He died of pneumonia he caught at his inauguration. Solve this puzzle to discover the year President Harrison was born.

- My hundreds and tens digits are the same; their sum is 14 and their product is 49.
- My units digit plus 4 is equal to my tens digit.
- The sum of all of my digits is equal to 3 x 3 x 2.

What year am I? ___ ___ ___ ___

Thousands Hundreds Tens Units

 # February 10th

On February 10th of this year the first singing telegram was delivered. Do you know what a telegram is? Solve this problem to find the year this greeting was delivered.

- My tens and units digits are the same number; their product is equal to my hundreds digit; their sum is 6.
- The sum of all of my digits = 32 ÷ 2.

What year am I? ___ ___ ___ ___

Thousands Hundreds Tens Units

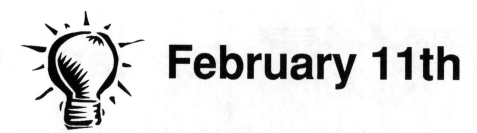

February 11th

February 11th is the birthday of Thomas Alva Edison. He invented the light bulb and more than 1,200 other things. He once said, "Genius is 1% inspiration and 99% perspiration." To find the year Edison was born, just solve this puzzle.

- My units digit plus 1 equals my hundreds digit.
- My tens digit is the same as the number of quarts in one gallon.
- The product of my hundreds and tens digit is 32.
- The sum of all of my digits is a multiple of 10 and 2.

What year am I? ____ ____ ____ ____

                      Thousands Hundreds Tens Units

February 12th

On February 12th of this year Abraham Lincoln, the 16th president of the U.S., was born in Kentucky. He was assassinated on Good Friday when he was 56 years old. To find out when Lincoln was born, just solve this puzzle.

- My hundreds digit is the same as the number of sides in an octagon.
- My units digit is one more than my hundreds digit.
- My tens digit is one less than my thousands digit.
- The sum of all of my digits is the same as the volume of a box: length of 2, width of 3, and height of 3.

What year am I? ____ ____ ____ ____

                      Thousands Hundreds Tens Units

What Year am I?

February 13th

On February 13th of this year the first public school was opened in America. It was named the Boston Latin School. To find the year of its opening, just solve this puzzle.

- The two digit number formed by my thousands and hundreds digit is the quotient: $80 \div 5$.
- My tens digit is the missing number in this sequence: 1, 1, 2, ____, 5, 8, 13, 21 . . .
- My date is divisible by 5 but not 10.

What year am I? __ __ __ __

Thousands Hundreds Tens Units

February 14th

On February 14th of this year, Arizona became the 48th state of the U.S. To learn the year, just solve this puzzle.

- The two-digit number formed by my tens and units digit is the number of inches in one foot.
- My hundreds digit is three times the sum of my tens and units digits.
- The sum of all of my digits is the difference between 558 and 545.

What year am I? __ __ __ __

Thousands Hundreds Tens Units

February 15th

On February 15th Pedro Menendez De Aviles, the Spanish explorer, was born. He explored the coast of Florida and set up a fort at St. Augustine. To find out when this great sailor was born, just solve this puzzle.

- My thousands and hundreds digits have a sum of 6 and a product that's only 5!
- My units digit is the same as the number of sides in a nonagon.
- My thousands and tens digits are the same.
- The sum of all of my digits is equal to $48 \div 3$.

What year am I? $\underline{\qquad}$ $\underline{\qquad}$ $\underline{\qquad}$ $\underline{\qquad}$
Thousands Hundreds Tens Units

February 16th

February 16th is the birthday of Edgar Bergen, a ventriloquist, who was the voice of Charlie McCarthy, Mortimer Snerd, and Effie Klinker. To find out the year Bergen was born, solve this puzzle.

- My units digit is 1/3 of my hundreds digit; both are odd numbers.
- My tens digit is one less than my thousands digit.
- The sum of all of my digits is $1 + (4 \times 3)$.

What year am I? $\underline{\qquad}$ $\underline{\qquad}$ $\underline{\qquad}$ $\underline{\qquad}$
Thousands Hundreds Tens Units

   What Year am I?

February 17th

On February 17th of this year Geronimo, the Native American leader, died at Fort Sill, Oklahoma. He was the chief of the Chiricahua Apache tribe. To learn the year of his death, just solve this puzzle.

- My hundreds digit and units digit are the same; their sum is 18 and their product is 81.
- My tens digit is one less than my thousands digit.
- The sum of my digits is the difference between 1601 and 1582.

What year am I? __ __ __ __
Thousands   Hundreds   Tens   Units

February 18th

On February 18th of this year "Ollie" became the first cow to fly in an airplane. During the flight she was milked and the milk was put in paper containers. Ollie, the cow, was then parachuted over St. Louis, Missouri. To find the date of Ollie's adventure, just solve this puzzle.

- The two-digit number formed by my tens and units digit is the same as the number of inches in 2 1/2 feet.
- My hundreds digit is three times my tens digit — both numbers are odd.
- The sum of all of my digits is one more than the number of inches in one foot.

What year am I? __ __ __ __
Thousands   Hundreds   Tens   Units

February 19th

February 19th is the birthday of the Polish astronomer, Nicolaus Copernicus. The Copernican Theory said the sun (not the earth) was at the center of our system of planets. Solve this problem to find the year Copernicus was born.

- My units digit is the number of sides on a triangle.
- My hundreds digit is the same as the number of quarts in one gallon.
- My tens digit is in the hundred-millions place in this number: 2,746,890,511.
- The sum of all of my digits is same as the number of nickels in 75¢.

What year am I? ___ ___ ___ ___
                Thousands Hundreds Tens Units

February 20th

On February 20th of this year the first toothpick–manufacturing machine was patented. Solve this problem to discover the year.

- My tens digit is one less than my hundreds digit.
- The product of my tens and hundreds digits is 56.
- My units digit is the number of pints in one quart.
- The sum of all of my digits is equal to the number of inches in 1 1/2 feet.

What year am I? ___ ___ ___ ___
                Thousands Hundreds Tens Units

28   What Year am I?

February 21st

On February 21st of this year popcorn was first introduced to the American settlers. To find out the year this delicious snack was discovered, solve this puzzle.

- Look at the number 2,463,715. My hundreds digit is the digit in the ten-thousands place of this number.
- My tens digit is 1/2 of my hundreds digit.
- My hundreds digit is the same as the number of sides in a hexagon.
- The sum of all of my digits is equal to the number of dimes in $1.00.

What year am I? ___ ___ ___ ___
Thousands Hundreds Tens Units

February 22nd

On February 22nd George Washington, the first president of the U.S., celebrates his birthday. To discover the year he was born, just solve this puzzle.

- The two-digit number formed by my tens and units digits could be the volume of a box with a width of 4, a depth of 4, and a height of 2.
- My hundreds digit is the average of 12, 5, 8, and 3.
- The sum of all of my digits is the missing number in this problem: 52 ÷ 4 = ☐.

What year am I? ___ ___ ___ ___
Thousands Hundreds Tens Units

         What Year am I?

February 23rd

On February 23rd of this year the American flag was raised on Mt. Surabachi, Iwo Jima, by the U.S. Marines. To learn the year, solve this puzzle.

- The sum of my tens and units digits is equal to my hundreds digit; their product is 20.
- My tens digit is one less than my units digit.
- The sum of all of my digits is 19.

What year am I? _____ _____ _____ _____

Thousands Hundreds Tens Units

February 24th

On February 24th of this year Wilhelm Karl Grimm, one of the Brothers Grimm and author of *Grimm's Fairy Tales*, was born. To learn the year, solve this puzzle.

- My tens digit is the same as the number of sides on an octagon.
- My hundreds digit is one less than my tens digit.
- My units digit is the number of inches in 1/2 of a foot.
- The sum of all of my digits is 22.

What year am I? _____ _____ _____ _____

Thousands Hundreds Tens Units

What Year am I?

February 25th

On February 25th of this year the French painter Pierre Auguste Renoir was born. To find the year Renoir was born, solve this puzzle.

- My thousands and units digits are the same.
- My hundreds digit is twice the size of my tens digit.
- My tens digit is the number given to the month of April.
- The sum of all of my digits is the difference between 1303 and 1289.

What year am I? ___ ___ ___ ___
　　　　　　　　Thousands　Hundreds　Tens　Units

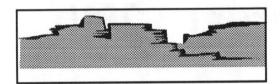

February 26th

On February 26th of this year the Grand Canyon National Park was established. This natural wonder covers 1,218,375 square acres of land in Arizona. To find the year it became a national park, solve this puzzle.

- The two-digit number formed by my thousands and hundreds digit is the same as the two-digit number formed by my tens and units digits.
- My units digit minus 8 is equal to my tens digit.
- The sum of all of my digits is the same as the number of nickels in $1.00.

What year am I? ___ ___ ___ ___
　　　　　　　　Thousands　Hundreds　Tens　Units

　　　　　　31　　　　　　What Year am I?

February 27th

On February 27th of this year Henry Wadsworth Longfellow was born. Have you heard the poem "Paul Revere's Ride"? To find the year Longfellow was born, solve this puzzle.

- My hundreds digit is the same as the perimeter of this diagram: ▭▭▭
- My tens digit is the product of 6x9x6x0x2x1.
- My units digit is one less than my hundreds digit.
- The sum of my date is a multiple of 2, 4, and 8.

What year am I? ___ ___ ___ ___

             Thousands Hundreds Tens Units

M*A*S*H

February 28th

On February 28th of this year the last episode of **M*A*S*H** appeared on television. It was on the air for 11 years and had more than 255 shows. To find the year this episode aired, just solve this problem.

- The Least Common Multiple of my tens and units digits is 24; their difference is 5.
- My hundreds digit is three times the size of my units digit.
- My units digit is the smallest odd prime number.
- The sum of all of my digits is the product of 7 and 3.

What year am I? ___ ___ ___ ___

             Thousands Hundreds Tens Units

February 29th

February 29th is John P. Holland's birthday. He invented the submarine. To find out the year of this "underwater" invention, solve this problem.

- The tens and units digits are the same number; their sum is 8 and their product is 16.
- The two-digit number formed by my thousands and hundreds digits is the quotient: 54 ÷ 3.

What year am I? ___ ___ ___ ___

Thousands   Hundreds   Tens   Units

What Year am I?

March 1st

On March 1st of this year President John F. Kennedy signed an executive order which formed the Peace Corps. Since that year the Corps has sent more than 150,000 volunteers to help people in poor countries. Solve this puzzle to find what year this happened.

- My thousands and units digit are the same number.
- My hundreds digit minus 3 is equal to my tens digit.
- The product of my hundreds digit and 8 is 72.
- The sum of all of my digits is a prime number.

What year am I? ___ ___ ___ ___

Thousands   Hundreds   Tens   Units

 # March 2nd

On March 2nd of this year Theodor Geisel, "Dr. Seuss," was born. Among his creations were, *The Cat in the Hat* and *The Grinch Who Stole Christmas*. What else did he write? To find the year Dr. Seuss was born, solve this puzzle.

- My units digit is the same as the number of sides in a quadrilateral.
- The sum of my thousands and tens digits is 1.
- The sum of all of my digits is 14.

What year am I? ___ ___ ___ ___

Thousands   Hundreds   Tens   Units

 What Year am I?

March 3rd

On March 3rd of this year Alexander Graham Bell was born. He invented the telephone, the phonograph, and phonograph records. Solve this puzzle to find the year that Mr. Bell was born.

- My thousands digit plus my units digit is equal to my hundreds digit.
- My hundreds digit is the same as the number of sides in an octagon.
- My tens digit is 1/2 of my hundreds digit.
- The sum of all of my digits is the missing number: ☐ x 5 = 100.

What year am I? __ __ __ __

Thousands   Hundreds   Tens   Units

March 4th

March 4th is the birthday of Casimir Pulaski, the American Revolutionary War hero. A Polish military leader, he joined General Washington to fight the British. To discover the year he was born, solve this puzzle.

- My hundreds and units digit are the same number; their sum is 14 and their product is 49.
- My tens digit is equal to my hundreds digit minus 3.
- If you divide my hundreds digit divided by my tens digit you will get a remainder of 3.
- The sum of all of my digits is 19.

What year am I? __ __ __ __

Thousands   Hundreds   Tens   Units

March 5th

March 5th of this year was the first time the International Day of the Seal was celebrated. Congress wanted to draw attention to the cruelty of seal hunts. Zoos all over the world celebrate this day with special programs. Discover the year this celebration started by solving this puzzle.

- My units digit is the ten-thousands place in this number: 1,628,903.
- My tens digit is in the thousands place.
- My hundreds digit is the area of this square: ■ 3
- The sum of my digits is the value of 4 nickels.

What year am I? ___ ___ ___ ___

Thousands Hundreds Tens Units

Alamo

March 6th

March 6th is the anniversary of the fall of the Texas fort the Alamo. The siege was led by General Santa Anna. Solve this puzzle to find the year the Alamo fell.

- The product of my tens and units digits is 18; their sum is 9.
- My tens digit is 1/2 of my units digit.
- My hundreds digit is the missing number: $128 \div \square = 16$.
- The sum of all of my digits is 18.

What year am I? ___ ___ ___ ___

Thousands Hundreds Tens Units

March 7th

On March 7th of this year President Woodrow Wilson approved a new bronze medal for distinguished service during war. To find out the year this award was approved, just solve this puzzle.

- My thousands and tens digit are the same number.
- My units digit plus 1 equals my hundreds digit.
- My hundreds digit is the missing number in this problem: □ x 12 = 108.
- The sum of all of my digits is 19.

What year am I? ___ ___ ___ ___

        Thousands Hundreds Tens Units

March 8th

On March 8th of this year the first dog license law was passed in the United States. It was passed in New York. To find out the year, solve this puzzle.

- My date is divisible by 2.
- My hundreds digit is twice the size of my units digit.
- My units digit is the same as the number of sides in a quadrilateral.
- My tens digit is one more than my hundreds digit.
- The sum of all of my digits is the product of 11 and 2.

What year am I? ___ ___ ___ ___

        Thousands Hundreds Tens Units

          What Year am I?

March 9th

March 9th is the birthday of Amerigo Vespucci. Born in Florence, Italy, he was the navigator for whom the Americas were named. Solve this puzzle to discover the year Amerigo was born.

- The two-digit number formed by my hundreds and tens digit is the Least Common Multiple of 9 and 5.
- My thousands and units digits are the same.
- The sum of my digits is the perimeter of this figure:

What year am I? ___ ___ ___ ___

Thousands Hundreds Tens Units

March 10th

On March 10th of this year paper money was first issued in the U.S. The denominations were $5, $10, and $20.

- My hundreds digit is the sum of my tens and units digits.
- My units digit is the only even prime number.
- My hundreds digit is the average of these numbers: 15 + 4 + 9 + 5 + 7.
- The sum of all of my digits is 17.

What year am I? ___ ___ ___ ___

Thousands Hundreds Tens Units

What Year am I?

March 11th

On March 11th of this year Johnny Appleseed died. His real name was John Chapman and he really did plant apple orchards. The Indians thought he was a great medicine man because of his love of animals and nature. To learn the year he died, just solve this puzzle.

- My tens digit is 1/2 of my hundreds digit.
- My units digit is one less than my hundreds digit.
- The sum of my units digit and tens digits is 11; their product is 28.
- The sum of my digits is the same as two decades.

What year am I? __ __ __ __

Thousands   Hundreds   Tens   Units

March 12th

On March 12th of this year the Girl Scouts of America was founded by Juliette Low in Savannah, Georgia. To find out the year, just solve this puzzle.

- The two-digit number formed by my tens and units digits is equal to the product of 6 and 2.
- My hundreds digit is the missing factor of 36:
  1, 2, 3, 4, 6, ____, 12, 18, 36.
- The sum of all of my digits is 39 ÷ 3.

What year am I? __ __ __ __

Thousands   Hundreds   Tens   Units

39

What Year am I?

March 13th

On March 13th of this year the planet Uranus was discovered by Sir William Herschel. The 7th planet from the sun, it takes 84 years to orbit the sun. To find out the year of this discovery, solve this puzzle.

- My thousands and units digits are the same.
- My hundreds digit is one less than my tens digit.
- My tens digit is the same as the number of sides in an octagon.
- The sum of all of my digits is 17.

What year am I? ___ ___ ___ ___

Thousands Hundreds Tens Units

March 14th

March 14th is Albert Einstein's birthday. Born in Germany, he won the Nobel Prize. To find the year he was born, just solve this puzzle.

- My tens digit is one less than my hundreds digit.
- My units digit is one more than my hundreds digit.
- The product of my tens and units digits is 63; their sum is 16.
- The sum of all of my digits is the difference between 715 and 690.

What year am I? ___ ___ ___ ___

Thousands Hundreds Tens Units

What Year am I?

Maine

March 15th

On March 15th of this year Maine became the 23rd state. To find the year, just solve this puzzle.

- My date is divisible by 2, 5, and 10.
- My hundreds digit is four times my tens digit.
- Find the average of 12, 6, 10, 3, and 9 and you will have my hundreds digit.
- The sum of my digits is the quotient of $143 \div 13$.

What year am I? ___ ___ ___ ___

Thousands Hundreds Tens Units

March 16th

March 16th is known as "Black Press Day" because the first Black newspaper in the U.S., *Freedom's Journal*, was founded in New York. Discover the year; solve this puzzle.

- The two-digit number formed by my tens and units digits is a multiple of 3 and 9.
- My tens digit is 1/4 of my hundreds digit.
- My hundreds digit is one more than my units digit.
- The sum of all of my digits is the product of 6 and 3.

What year am I? ___ ___ ___ ___

Thousands Hundreds Tens Units

March 17th

On March 17th of this year the Campfire Girls of America was organized. The group's watchword, **WOHELO,** stands for the words, "work," "health," and "love." To find out the year, just solve this puzzle.

- The two-digit number formed by my tens and units digits is the missing factor in □ x 3 = 36.
- My hundreds digit is the same as the number of sides in a nonagon.
- The sum of my digits is one less than the product of 7 and 2.

What year am I? ___ ___ ___ ___

          Thousands Hundreds   Tens   Units

March 18th

On March 18th of this year the first electric razor was sold by Schick, Inc. To find the year, just solve this puzzle.

- My thousands and units digits are the same number.
- My hundreds digit is three times my tens digit.
- My tens digit is the same as the number of sides in a triangle.

What year am I? ___ ___ ___ ___

          Thousands Hundreds   Tens   Units

March 19th

March 19th is the day that thousands of swallows return to San Juan Capistrano, California from their winter home in the South. Solve this problem to find the year the swallows first made this trip.

- My unit digit is the same as the number of sides in a hexagon.
- The product of my hundreds and tens digit is 49.
- The sum of my digits is equal to my hundreds digit times 3.

What year am I? ___ ___ ___ ___
Thousands Hundreds Tens Units

March 20th

On March 20th of this year we began our celebration of Earth Day — a day to think about our Earth and our environment. Solve this problem to discover the year we began this celebration.

- My hundreds and units digits are the same. Their product is 81.
- My tens digit is two less than my hundreds digit. It is a prime number.
- My sum is the average of 25, 32, and 21.

What year am I? ___ ___ ___ ___
Thousands Hundreds Tens Units

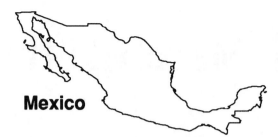

Mexico

March 21st

March 21st is the birthday of Benito Pablo Juarez, a symbol of freedom to the people of Mexico. To find the year he was born, solve this puzzle.

- Look at the number 45,015. My tens digit is the same as the digit in the hundreds place of this number.
- My units digit is 6 greater than my tens digit.
- My hundreds digit is the area of this rectangle:

- The sum of all of my digits is equal to 15.

What year am I? ___ ___ ___ ___
              Thousands Hundreds Tens Units

March 22nd

March 22nd is William Shatner's birthday. He played Captain Kirk in the original *Star Trek*. He was born in Montreal, Quebec, Canada. To discover the year he was born, just solve this puzzle.

- Look at this number: 2,437,901. My tens digit is the same as the digit in the ten-thousands place.
- My hundreds digit is the same as the digit in this numbers hundred's place.
- The sum of all of my digits is the missing number in this problem: ☐ x 4 = 56.

What year am I? ___ ___ ___ ___
              Thousands Hundreds Tens Units

March 23rd

March 23rd is known as "Liberty Day" because it is the anniversary of Patrick Henry's speech, "I know not what course others may take, but as for me, give me liberty or give me death." To find out what year he made this famous speech, just solve this puzzle.

- My date is divisible by 5 but not 10.
- My hundreds and tens digits could be the sides of a square with a perimeter of 28.
- The sum of all of my digits is the same as the number of nickels in $1.

What year am I? __ __ __ __

Thousands   Hundreds   Tens   Units

March 24th

On March 24th of this year the *Exxon Valdez* ship ran aground in Prince William Sound, Alaska, causing a horrible oil spill. The ship leaked 11 million gallons of oil and did terrible damage to both the land and wildlife. Solve this puzzle to discover the year of this ecological disaster.

- My hundreds and units digits are the same number; their product is 81.
- My tens digit is one less than my units digit.
- 567 ÷ 21 equals the sum of all of my digits.

What year am I? __ __ __ __

Thousands   Hundreds   Tens   Units

What Year am I?

March 25th

On March 25th of this year production of colored television sets began. To find the year, solve this puzzle.

- The two-digit number formed by my tens and units digits is the product of 9 and 6.
- My hundreds digit is equal to the sum of my tens and units digits.
- The sum of my digits is the perimeter of this triangle:

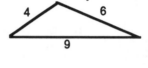

What year am I? ___ ___ ___ ___

Thousands Hundreds Tens Units

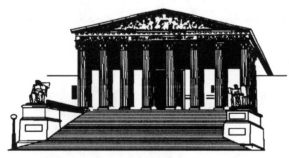

March 26th

March 26th is the birthday of Sandra Day O'Connor, the first woman appointed as a justice to the Supreme Court. To find the year she was born, solve this puzzle.

- My date is a multiple of 10.
- My tens digit is 1/3 of my hundreds digit.
- The sum of my digits is one more than the number of inches in one foot.

What year am I? ___ ___ ___ ___

Thousands Hundreds Tens Units

Alaska

March 27th

On March 27th of this year a very serious earthquake occurred at Prince William Sound, Alaska. It registered 8.5 on the Richter Scale, lasted for seven minutes, and opened cracks on the earth 3 feet wide and 40 feet deep!

- My units digit is the same as the area of this diagram:

- The sum of my tens and units digits is the same as its perimeter.
- My hundreds digit is the number of feet in 3 yards.
- The sum of my digits is the number of dimes in $2.

What year am I? ____ ____ ____ ____
Thousands Hundreds Tens Units

March 28th

On March 28th of this year the first washing machine in the U.S. was patented by Nathaniel Briggs. To find the year, just solve this puzzle.

- My hundreds and units digits are the same number; it is the largest single-digit prime number.
- My tens digit is the largest single-digit number.
- The sum of all of my digits is the same as two dozen.

What year am I? ____ ____ ____ ____
Thousands Hundreds Tens Units

Oscar Mayer Wiener

March 29th

March 29th is the birthday of Oscar Mayer, the founder of the famous hotdog company.

- The two-digit number formed by my thousands and hundreds digits is the perimeter of this figure:

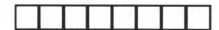

- My tens digit is three less than my hundreds digit.
- My units digit is the equal to the sum of my thousands and hundreds digit.

What year am I? ___ ___ ___ ___

  Thousands Hundreds Tens Units

Alaska

March 30th

On March 30th of this year the U.S. purchased Alaska from the Russians. To find out the date of this purchase, solve this puzzle.

- Look at this number: 157,680,000
- My units digit is in the millions place.
- My tens digit is in the hundred-thousands place.
- My hundreds digit is in the ten-thousands place.
- The sum of all of my digits is the quotient of 88 and 4.

What year am I? ___ ___ ___ ___

  Thousands Hundreds Tens Units

What Year am I?

March 31st

March 31st was the birthday of Robert von Bunsen, the inventor of the Bunsen burner. This heat source is used by chemistry students all over the world. To discover the year he was born, solve this puzzle.

- My thousands, tens, and units digits are the same.
- The sum of my thousands, tens, and units digits is 3.
- The sum of all of my digits is worth a penny more than a dime.

What year am I? ___ ___ ___ ___

Thousands Hundreds Tens Units

What Year am I?

April 1st

On April 1st of this year the first movie censorship board was set up. Solve this puzzle to find what year movies first had a rating.

- My hundreds digit is three times my units digit.
- All of my digits are odd numbers.
- My thousands and tens digits are the same.
- The sum of all of my digits is the quotient of $112 \div 8$.

What year am I? __ __ __ __

               Thousands Hundreds Tens Units

April 2nd

On April 2nd of this year Frederic Auguste Betholdi created *Liberty Enlightening the World*, better known as the Statue of Liberty.

- My units digit is the same as the number of quarts in one gallon.
- My tens digits is the same as the number of feet in one yard.
- My hundreds digit is the number of sides in an octagon.
- The sum of all of my digits is 16.

What year am I? __ __ __ __

               Thousands Hundreds Tens Units

April 3rd

April 3rd is Washington Irving's birthday. Irving wrote *Rip Van Winkle* and *The Legend of Sleepy Hollow*. To find the year he was born, just solve this puzzle.

- My thousands digit plus my hundreds digit is equal to my tens digit.
- My units digit is the average of 4, 5, 1, 2, and 3.
- The sum of my hundreds and tens digit is 15.
- The sum of all of my digits is the missing number:
  $\square \times 3 = 57$.

What year am I? ___ ___ ___ ___

Thousands Hundreds Tens Units

April 4th

April 4th is the anniversary of the year Congress approved the first flag for the U.S. by passing the Flag Act.

- My two-digit number formed by the thousands and hundreds digits is the same as the two-digit number formed by my tens and units digits.
- My hundreds and units digits are the number in sides an octagon.
- The sum of all of my digits is the same as the number of inches in 1 1/2 feet.

What year am I? ___ ___ ___ ___

Thousands Hundreds Tens Units

April 5th

April 5th is Booker T. Washington's birthday. A Black leader he said, "No race can prosper till it learns there is as much dignity in tilling a field as in writing a poem."

- My units digit is in the hundred-thousands place of this number: 1,625,903
- My tens digit is in the thousands place of the same number.
- My hundreds digit is the area of this rectangle:

- The sum of my digits is the same as two decades.

What year am I? ___ ___ ___ ___

          Thousands Hundreds Tens Units

April 6th

On April 6th of this year Robert E. Perry and Matthew Henson reached the North Pole. To find the year they reached their goal, solve this puzzle.

- My hundreds and units digits are the same; their product is 81.
- My tens digit is the millions digit of this number: 870,155,961
- My sum is the missing number: $95 \div \square = 5$.

What year am I? ___ ___ ___ ___

          Thousands Hundreds Tens Units

          52   What Year am I?

April 7th

April 7th is Ravi Shankar's birthday. He is an Indian musician who plays an unusual instrument, the sitar. It is made from a gourd and is like a lute. To find out the year Shankar was born, just solve this puzzle.

- My date is a multiple of 10.
- My tens digit is the number of pints in one quart.
- My hundreds digit is the missing number in this problem: $\square$ x 12 = 108.
- The sum of all of my digits is 144 ÷ 12.

What year am I? ___ ___ ___ ___

Thousands Hundreds Tens Units

April 8th

On April 8th of this year the homerun record was set by Hank Aaron when he hit the 715th homerun of his career, breaking Babe Ruth's record. He finished his career with 755 homeruns. To find out the year Aaron set this record, just solve this puzzle.

- My date is divisible by 2.
- My hundreds digit is two more than my tens digit.
- The product of my hundreds and tens digits is 63.
- The sum of all of my digits is 21.

What year am I? ___ ___ ___ ___

Thousands Hundreds Tens Units

What Year am I?

April 9th

April 9th is the anniversary of Marion Anderson's outdoor Easter Concert. Because of prejudice she could not sing in a concert hall so she sang from the steps of the Lincoln Memorial. To learn the year of this concert, solve this puzzle.

- My hundreds and units digits are the same digit; their product is 81.
- My tens digit is 1/3 of my hundreds digit.
- The sum of my digits is the perimeter of this figure:

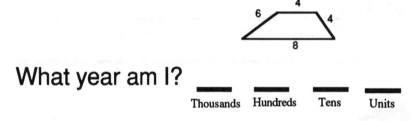

What year am I? __ __ __ __

Thousands Hundreds Tens Units

April 10th

On April 10th of this year William Booth was born. He founded the Salvation Army to help the sick and poor. To find the year Booth was born, just solve this puzzle.

- My hundreds digit is the same as my units digit; their sum is 16.
- My tens digit is the largest single-digit prime number.
- The sum of all of my digits is the number of hours in one day.

What year am I? __ __ __ __

Thousands Hundreds Tens Units

   What Year am I?

April 11th

April 11th is Jane Matilda Bolin's birthday. She was the first Black woman to graduate from the Yale School of Law and went on to become the first Black woman judge in the U.S. To find the year she was born, just solve this puzzle.

- My tens digit is one less than my thousands digit.
- My units digit is one less than my hundreds digit.
- The sum of my units digit and hundreds digit is 17; their product is 72.
- The sum of all of my digits is the difference between 432 and 414.

What year am I? ___ ___ ___ ___

Thousands Hundreds Tens Units

April 12th

April 12th is the anniversary of the "big wind." The highest-velocity wind ever recorded happened on this date at Mt. Washington Observatory. Gusts reached 231 mph. To find out the year, just solve this puzzle.

- The two-digit number formed by my tens and units digits is equal to the product of 17 and 2.
- My hundreds digit is the missing factor of 36:
  1, 2, 3, 4, 6, ___ , 12, 18, 36.
- The sum of all of my digits is 68 ÷ 4.

What year am I? ___ ___ ___ ___

Thousands Hundreds Tens Units

What Year am I?

April 13th

April 13th is the anniversary of the Great Chicago Flood. When the Chicago River broke through an underground tunnel wall, millions of gallons of water flooded the downtown area of Chicago. To find out the year this happened, solve this puzzle.

- My hundreds and tens digits could be the sides of this square:  Area = 81 .
- My units digit is the only even prime number.
- My sum is the average of 30, 13, and 20.

What year am I? ___ ___ ___ ___
Thousands Hundreds Tens Units

April 14th

April 14th is the birthday of Anne Sullivan, the teacher who became famous for her work with Helen Keller. To find the year this great teacher was born, solve this puzzle.

- My tens and units digits are the same; their sum is 12 and their product is 36.
- My hundreds digit is two less than the number of years in a decade.
- The sum of all of my digits is the same as the number of days in three weeks.

What year am I? ___ ___ ___ ___
Thousands Hundreds Tens Units

April 15th

April 15th is Leonardo da Vinci's birthday. An Italian artist, his most famous painting was the *Mona Lisa*. To find the year da Vinci was born, solve this puzzle.

- My units digit is the number of pints in one quart.
- My hundreds digit is two times my units digit.
- My tens digit times itself is 25.
- My sum is the average of 15, 8, and 13.

What year am I? ___ ___ ___ ___

Thousands Hundreds Tens Units

April 16th

April 16th is Wilbur Wright's birthday. One of the famous Wright Brothers, he was the first to fly a plane at Kitty Hawk, North Carolina. Discover the year by solving this puzzle.

- My units digit is the number of days in one week.
- My tens digit is the same as the number of sides in a hexagon.
- My hundreds digit is two more than my tens digit.
- The sum of all of my digits is 22.

What year am I? ___ ___ ___ ___

Thousands Hundreds Tens Units

April 17th

On April 17th of this year the first law requiring fire escapes on apartment buildings was passed. To find out the year, just solve this puzzle.

- The two digit number formed by my tens and units digits is the number of months in five years.
- My hundreds digit is two more than my tens digit.
- The sum of my digits is the product of 5 and 3.

What year am I? ___ ___ ___ ___
Thousands Hundreds Tens Units

California

April 18th

April 18th is the anniversary of the great San Francisco earthquake. Nearly 4,000 people lost their lives. To find the year, just solve this puzzle.

- My thousands digit is one more than my tens digit.
- My date is divisible by 2.
- My hundreds digit is the same as the number of sides in a nonagon.
- My units digit is the same as the number of sides in a hexagon.

What year am I? ___ ___ ___ ___
Thousands Hundreds Tens Units

What Year am I?

April 19th

On April 19th of this year the Revolutionary War began. Did you know it ended eight years later on the exact same date, April 19th? To find the year the war started, solve this puzzle.

- My hundreds and tens digits are the same: the number of days in one week.
- My date is odd and divisible by 5.
- The sum of my digits is equal to my units digit x 4.

What year am I? ___ ___ ___ ___

Thousands   Hundreds   Tens   Units

April 20th

April 20th is Daniel C. French's birthday. He was the American sculptor who created the Lincoln Memorial. To find the year French was born, solve this puzzle.

- My date is divisible by 10.
- My hundreds digit is the same as the number of quarts in two gallons.
- My tens digit is the number of pennies in one nickel.
- My sum is the average of 17, 12, and 13.

What year am I? ___ ___ ___ ___

Thousands   Hundreds   Tens   Units

April 21st

April 21st is celebrated as "Kindergarten Day" because it's the birthday of Fredrich Froebel, who started the first kindergarten. To learn the year, solve this puzzle.

- Look at the number: 982,345,671.
- My tens digit is the same as the digit in the ten-millions place of this number.
- My units digit is the digit in the millions place.
- My hundreds digit is the digit in the tens place.
- The sum of my digits is the area of this rectangle:

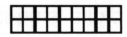

What year am I? ___ ___ ___ ___
                Thousands Hundreds Tens Units

April 22nd

On April 22nd of this year Babe Ruth made his pitching debut. He allowed six hits, got two singles, and shut out the Buffalo Bisons, 6 – 0. To discover the year of this game, solve this puzzle.

- The two-digit number formed by my tens and units digits is the number of days in two weeks.
- The two-digit number formed by my thousands and hundreds digit is the missing number in this problem: $4 \times \square = 76$.
- The sum of all of my digits is a multiple of 5.

What year am I? ___ ___ ___ ___
                Thousands Hundreds Tens Units

April 23rd

April 23rd is William Shakespeare's birthday. Born in England, he died on the exact same day he was born (April 23rd) 52 years later. To learn the year he was born, just solve this puzzle.

- My units digit is an even number and two less than my tens digit.
- The two-digit number formed by my hundreds and tens digits is the area of this rectangle: [8]⁷
- The sum of all of my digits is four more than the number of inches in a foot.

What year am I? ___ ___ ___ ___
Thousands Hundreds Tens Units

April 24th

On April 24th of this year the Library of Congress was started. It is now one of the greatest libraries in the world. Solve this puzzle to discover the year it was started.

- My date is divisible by 100.
- The two-digit number formed by my thousands and hundreds digit is the same as the number of inches in $1\frac{1}{2}$ feet.
- $144 \div 16$ equals the sum of all of my digits.

What year am I? ___ ___ ___ ___
Thousands Hundreds Tens Units

         What Year am I?

April 25th

On April 25th of this year the first seeing-eye dog in America was given to a blind person. Purebred female German shepherds are said to make the best seeing-eye dogs. To find the year, solve this puzzle.

- The two-digit number formed by my tens and units digit is the average of 19, 20, 17 and 36.
- My hundreds digit is the number assigned to the month of September.
- The sum of my digits is the perimeter of this triangle:

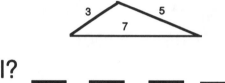

What year am I? ___ ___ ___ ___

Thousands   Hundreds   Tens   Units

The Richter Scale

April 26th

April 26th is the birthday of Charles Richter. He developed the scale that tells us how powerful an earthquake is. To find the year he was born, solve this puzzle.

- My date is a multiple of 100.
- The sum of my thousands and hundreds digits is the number of dimes in $1.
- The sum of my digits is two less than the number of inches in one foot.

What year am I? ___ ___ ___ ___

Thousands   Hundreds   Tens   Units

What Year am I?

April 27th

April 27th is Walter Lantz's birthday. He is the cartoonist who created Woody Woodpecker. Solve this puzzle to learn the year he was born.

- The three-digit number formed by my hundreds, tens, and units digits is the same as nine centuries.
- The sum of my digits is the number of dimes in $1.

What year am I? __ __ __ __

Thousands Hundreds Tens Units

April 28th

April 28th is Jay Leno's birthday. This host of TV's *Tonight Show* was born in New Rochelle, New York. To learn the year, just solve this puzzle.

- My date is even and divisible by 10.
- My tens digit is the same as the number if sides on a pentagon.
- My hundreds digit is four more than my tens digit.
- The sum of my digits is the missing number:
  $\square \div 3 = 5$

What year am I? __ __ __ __

Thousands Hundreds Tens Units

What Year am I?

April 29th

April 29th is the birthday of Duke Ellington, the first to start the jazz big bands. He wrote more than 1,000 songs. One of his most famous was *Mood Indigo*. To learn the year he was born, solve this puzzle.

- The two-digit number formed by my thousands and hundreds digits the perimeter of this figure:

  ☐☐☐☐☐☐☐☐

- My tens and units digits are the same; their sum is 18 but their product is 81.
- The sum of all of my digits is a multiple of 9 and 3.

What year am I? ___ ___ ___ ___

<small>Thousands Hundreds Tens Units</small>

Louisiana

April 30th

On April 30th of this year Louisiana became the 18th state of the U.S. To find out the date, solve this puzzle.

- My two-digit number formed by my tens and units digits is the number of inches in a foot.
- My hundreds digit is the number of inches in 2/3 of a foot.
- The sum of all of my digits is $108 \div 9 =$

What year am I? ___ ___ ___ ___

<small>Thousands Hundreds Tens Units</small>

What Year am I?

May 1st

On May 1st of this year the Empire State Building was dedicated in New York City. It was the tallest building in the world for over 30 years. Solve this puzzle to find the year.

- My thousands and units digits are the same number.
- My tens digit is 1/3 of my hundreds digit.
- The sum of all of my digits is the number of days in two weeks.

What year am I? __ __ __ __

Thousands Hundreds Tens Units

May 2nd

On May 2nd of this year Catherine the Great, Empress of Russia, was born. To find the year she was born, solve this puzzle.

- My units digit is two more than my hundreds digit.
- My hundreds digit is the number of days in one week.
- My tens digit is the only even prime number.
- The sum of all of my digits is 19.

What year am I? __ __ __ __

Thousands Hundreds Tens Units

Israel

May 3rd

On May 3rd of this year Golda Meir, the former prime minister of Israel, was born in Milwaukee, Wisconsin. Solve this puzzle to find the year that she was born.

- My thousands digit plus my hundreds digit is equal to my tens digit.
- My units digit has 1, 2, and 4 as factors.
- The product of my hundreds and units digits is 64; their sum is 16.
- The sum of all of my digits is the missing number: $\square \times 2 = 52$.

What year am I? ___ ___ ___ ___

           Thousands Hundreds Tens Units

May 4th

May 4th is the birthday of Audrey Hepburn. She made 26 movies and received 4 Oscar nominations. She traveled around the world to raise money for the U.N. Children's Fund. To find the year she was born, just solve this puzzle.

- My hundreds and units digits are the same number; their product is 81.
- My tens digit is equal to my hundreds digit minus 7.
- The sum of my digits is equal to the number of days in 3 weeks.

What year am I? ___ ___ ___ ___

           Thousands Hundreds Tens Units

May 5th

May 5th is the day of the Mexican holiday Cinco de Mayo. It is the anniversary of the Battle of Puebla, at which the Mexicans defeated Napoleon III. Discover the year this celebration started by solving this puzzle.

- My units digit is the ten-thousands place in this number: 1,628,903
- My tens digit is in the hundred-thousands place of that same number.
- My hundreds digit is in the thousands place.
- The sum of all of my digits is the value of one dime, one nickel, and two pennies.

What year am I? ____ ____ ____ ____

Thousands Hundreds Tens Units

May 6th

May 6th is the anniversary of the Hindenburg disaster. After crossing the Atlantic the dirigible exploded over New Jersey. Do you know what a dirigible is? To find out the year this accident occurred, solve this puzzle.

- The product of my tens and units digits is 21.
- My units digit is four greater than my tens digit.
- My hundreds digit is the missing number: $144 \div \square = 16$.
- The sum of all of my digits is two decades.

What year am I? ____ ____ ____ ____

Thousands Hundreds Tens Units

May 7th

May 7th is Johannes Brahms' birthday. Considered one of the world's greatest composers, Brahms wrote a famous lullaby that you probably know. To find the year he was born, solve this puzzle.

- My tens and units digits could be the sides of a square with an area of 9 square units.
- My hundreds digit is the missing number in this problem: □ x 12 = 96.
- The sum of all of my digits is 15.

What year am I? _____ _____ _____ _____

            Thousands Hundreds Tens   Units

May 8th

On May 8th of this year Hernando DeSoto was the first European to discover the Mississippi River. To find out the year of DeSoto's discovery, solve this puzzle.

- The sum of my hundreds and tens digits is 9; their product is 20.
- My hundreds digit is one more than my tens digit.
- My units digit is the first counting number.
- The sum of my digits is one more than a decade.

What year am I? _____ _____ _____ _____

            Thousands Hundreds Tens   Units

What Year am I?

May 9th

On May 9th of this year the first cartoon was published in America. To learn the year, solve this puzzle.

- The two-digit number formed by my tens and units digits is the product of 9 and 6.
- My hundreds digit is two more than my tens digit.
- The sum of my digits is the perimeter of this figure:

What year am I? ___ ___ ___ ___
 Thousands Hundreds Tens Units

May 10th

On May 10th of this year the first planetarium in the U.S. was opened on the lakefront in Chicago, Illinois. To learn the year, solve this puzzle.

- My tens digit is 1/3 of my hundreds digit.
- My date is even and divisible by 10.
- The sum of all of my digits is one more than the number of months in one year.

What year am I? ___ ___ ___ ___
 Thousands Hundreds Tens Units

Minnesota

May 11th

On May 11th of this year Minnesota became the 32nd state of the U. S. To learn the year, solve this puzzle.

- My hundreds and units digits are the same even number.
- My tens digit is the third prime number.
- The sum of my hundreds and units digit is 16; their product is 64.
- The sum of all of my digits is two years more than the number of years in two decades.

What year am I? ___ ___ ___ ___

       Thousands Hundreds Tens Units

May 12th

May 12th is Florence Nightingale's birthday. An English nurse, she is considered the mother of modern nursing. To find out the year, just solve this puzzle.

- The two-digit number formed by my tens and units digits is the same as the number of legs on 10 chickens.
- My hundreds digit is the missing number in this pattern: 2, 4, 6, __ , 10, 12.
- The sum of all of my digits is 33 ÷ 3.

What year am I? ___ ___ ___ ___

       Thousands Hundreds Tens Units

What Year am I?

 # May 13th

May 13th is the anniversary of the founding of Jamestown, the first permanent English colony in North America. To learn the year, solve this puzzle.

- My units digit is the number of days in one week.
- My hundreds digit is the number of feet in 72 inches.
- My tens digit is one less than my thousands digit.
- The sum of all of my digits is 2 more than the number of months in one year.

What year am I? ___ ___ ___ ___

Thousands Hundreds Tens Units

 # May 14th

May 14th is Gabriel Fahrenheit's birthday. He was the first to use mercury in thermometers. To find the year he was born, just solve this puzzle.

- My hundreds, tens, and units digits form a palindrome of all even numbers; its sum is 20.
- My units digit is two less than my tens digit.
- My hundreds digit is the same as the number of sides in a hexagon.
- The sum of all of my digits is the difference between 716 and 695.

What year am I? ___ ___ ___ ___

Thousands Hundreds Tens Units

   What Year am I?

May 15th

May 15th is Frank Baum's birthday. He is best known for writing *The Wonderful Wizard of Oz.* To find the year he was born, just solve this puzzle.

- My date is odd and divisible by 5.
- The sum of my thousands and hundreds digits is two times my units digit.
- My sum is the average of 12, 11, 10, 23, and 19.

What year am I? ___ ___ ___ ___
Thousands Hundreds Tens Units

May 16th

On May 16th of this year the U.S. minted the first 5¢ piece. Discover the year by solving this puzzle.

- The two-digit number formed by my tens and units digits is a multiple of 11 and 6.
- My hundreds digit is two more than my tens digit.
- The sum of my digits is the perimeter of this figure:

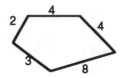

What year am I? ___ ___ ___ ___
Thousands Hundreds Tens Units

     What Year am I?

May 17th

On May 17th of this year the New York Stock Exchange was established. Two dozen merchants met under a cottonwood tree on Wall Street to conduct business. To find out the year, solve this puzzle.

- My units digit is the number of pints in one quart.
- My tens digit is two more than my hundreds digit.
- My hundreds digit is the same as the number of sides in a heptagon.
- The sum of my digits is 19.

What year am I? ___ ___ ___ ___

Thousands   Hundreds   Tens   Units

May 18th

May 18th is Pope John Paul II's birthday. He was born in Wadowice, Poland. To find the year, just solve this puzzle.

- My date is an even number and divisible by 10.
- My tens and units digits form a number that is 8 inches bigger than one foot.
- My hundreds digit is the same as the number of feet in 3 yards.
- The sum of my digits is the number of eggs in one dozen.

What year am I? ___ ___ ___ ___

Thousands   Hundreds   Tens   Units

May 19th

May 19th is the birthday of Malcolm X, a famous Black civil rights leader. He was assassinated while giving a speech in New York City. To find the year he was born, solve this puzzle.

- My tens and units digits form a two-digit number that could be the area of a square whose sides are 5.
- My hundreds digit could be the area of a square whose sides are 3.
- The sum of my digits is a decade plus 7.

What year am I? ___ ___ ___ ___

Thousands Hundreds Tens Units

May 20th

May 20th is Dolly Madison's birthday. The wife of our fourth president, she rescued many valuable papers and artwork from a fire that engulfed the White House. To discover the year she was born, solve this puzzle.

- My tens and units digits are consecutive even numbers whose sum is 14 and whose product is 48.
- My hundreds digit is one more than my tens digit and one less than my units digit.
- The sum of my digits is 22.

What year am I? ___ ___ ___ ___

Thousands Hundreds Tens Units

What Year am I?

May 21st

On May 21st of this year the Red Cross was founded by Clara Barton. The Red Cross provides disaster relief in the U.S. and other countries. To find the year it was founded, solve this puzzle.

- My date is a palindrome; it reads the same forwards and backwards.
- My hundreds digit is one greater than the number of days in a week.
- The sum of all of my digits is equal to 18.

What year am I? ___ ___ ___ ___
Thousands Hundreds Tens Units

May 22nd

May 22nd is Sir Arthur Conan Doyle's birthday. He is known for his Sherlock Holmes mysteries. To discover the year he was born, just solve this puzzle.

- Look at this number: 2,835,901. My tens digit is the same as the digit in the thousands place.
- My hundreds digit is the same as the digit in the hundred-thousands place.
- My units digit is the same as the digit in the hundreds place.
- My sum is the average of 30, 16, 24, and 22.

What year am I? ___ ___ ___ ___
Thousands Hundreds Tens Units

What Year am I?

May 23rd

Medal of Honor

On May 23rd of this year, Sgt. William Carney became the first Black American to win the Congressional Medal of Honor. To find out the year, just solve this puzzle.

- My hundreds, tens, and units digits form a three-digit number that is the same as the number of years in 9 centuries.
- The sum of my digits is the number assigned to the month of October.

What year am I? ___ ___ ___ ___

Thousands Hundreds Tens Units

May 24th

May 24th is the anniversary of the opening of the Brooklyn Bridge in New York. It is a steel suspension bridge with a span of 1595 feet. Solve this puzzle to discover the year of this opening.

- My units digit is the first odd prime number.
- My hundreds and tens digits are the same; their sum is 16 and their product is 64.
- 280 ÷ 14 equals the sum of all of my digits.

What year am I? ___ ___ ___ ___

Thousands Hundreds Tens Units

What Year am I?

May 25th

May 25th is the birthday of Bill "Bojangles" Robinson, the king of the tapdancers. To find the year he was born, solve this puzzle.

- The tens digit is the same as the number of days in one week.
- My hundreds and units digits are the same; they are the digit is the ten-millions place of this number:
  1,286,003,751.
- The sum of my digits is the same as two dozen.

What year am I? ___ ___ ___ ___

              Thousands Hundreds Tens Units

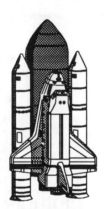

May 26th

May 26th is the birthday of Dr. Sally Kirsten Ride, an astronaut. She was the first woman in space. To find the year she was born, solve this puzzle.

- My thousands and units digits are the same.
- My tens digit is a factor of both 10 and 25.
- My hundreds digit is the perimeter of this polygon:

What year am I? ___ ___ ___ ___

              Thousands Hundreds Tens Units

 What Year am I?

May 27th

May 27th is Rachel Carson's birthday. She is a scientist who wrote *Silent Spring*, the book that warned everyone about how pesticides were destroying our environment. To find the year, just solve this puzzle.

- My units digit is the same as the area of this diagram:

- The sum of my thousands and hundreds digits is the same as the number of years in a decade.
- My tens digit is the first whole number.
- The sum of my digits is three more than the number of days in two weeks.

What year am I? ___ ___ ___ ___

Thousands   Hundreds   Tens   Units

  **May 28th**

On May 28th of this year the Dionne quintuplets, Marie, Cecille, Yvonne, Emilie, and Annette, were born. They were the first quints to survive. To find the year, solve this puzzle.

- My tens digit is 1/3 of my hundreds digit.
- My units digit is one more than my tens digit.
- The sum of my thousands and hundreds digits is the same as the number of years in a decade.
- The sum of all of my digits is 17.

What year am I? ___ ___ ___ ___

Thousands   Hundreds   Tens   Units

What Year am I?

Wisconsin

May 29th

On May 29th of this year, Wisconsin became the 30th state of the U.S. To discover the year, solve this puzzle.

- My hundreds and units digits are the same number; their sum is 16 and their product is 64.
- My tens digit is the same as the number of pints in one quart.
- The sum of all of my digits is the number of days in three weeks.

What year am I? __ __ __ __

Thousands Hundreds Tens Units

May 30th

On May 30th of this year the first daily newspaper, *The Pennsylvania Evening Post*, was issued in Philadelphia, Pennsylvania. To learn the year it was published, solve this puzzle.

- Look at this number: 102,357,690,840.
- My units digit is in the hundred-millions place of this number.
- My tens digit is in the hundreds place of this number.
- My hundreds digit is in the millions place of this number.
- The sum of my digits is the largest prime < 20.

What year am I? __ __ __ __

Thousands Hundreds Tens Units

What Year am I?

May 31st

May 31st was the birthday of Clint Eastwood. He is famous for the "Dirty Harry" movies. To discover the year he was born, solve this puzzle.

- My date is divisible by 2, 5, and 10.
- The hundreds digit is three times my tens digit.
- The sum of all of my digits is worth 3¢ more than a dime.

What year am I? $\underline{\qquad}$ $\underline{\qquad}$ $\underline{\qquad}$ $\underline{\qquad}$

Thousands Hundreds Tens Units

Kentucky

June 1st

On June 1st of this year Kentucky became the 15th state of the United States. Solve this puzzle to find what year this occurred.

- My units digit is the number of pints in one quart.
- My hundreds digit is the number of days in one week.
- My tens digit is two greater than my hundreds digit.
- The sum of all of my digits is the quotient of 95 ÷ 5.

What year am I? ___ ___ ___ ___
Thousands   Hundreds   Tens   Units

June 2nd

On June 2nd of this year American Indians were granted citizenship by the Congress. To find the year this happened, just solve this puzzle.

- The two-digit number formed by my tens and units digits is the number of months in two years.
- My hundreds digit is the number of sides in a nonagon.
- The sum of all of my digits is the value of three nickels and one penny.

What year am I? ___ ___ ___ ___
Thousands   Hundreds   Tens   Units

    81   What Year am I?

June 3rd

June 3rd is Jefferson Davis's birthday. He was the only president of the Confederate States of America. To find the year he was born, just solve this puzzle.

- My hundreds and units digits are the same; their sum is 16 and their product is 64.
- My tens digit is the product of 14, 52, 10, 0, and 65.
- The sum of all of my digits is the missing number:
  $\Box$ x 6 = 102.

What year am I? ___ ___ ___ ___

          Thousands Hundreds Tens Units

June 4th

June 4th is the birthday of King George III of England. He was king during the Revolutionary War in America. To learn the year he was born, just solve this puzzle.

- My tens digit is the number of sides of a triangle.
- My units digit is the number of sides in an octagon.
- My hundreds digit is a prime number > 5 and < 11.
- My sum is the average of 21 and 17.

What year am I? ___ ___ ___ ___

          Thousands Hundreds Tens Units

What Year am I?

June 5th

On June 5th of this year the first hot-air balloon flight took place in France. The balloon rose 1500 feet and landed after a ten-minute flight. To learn the year, just solve this puzzle.

- My units digit is in the hundred-thousands place of this number: 19,385,706.
- My tens digit is in its ten-thousands place.
- My hundreds digit is in its hundreds place.
- The sum of all of my digits is the two-digit number formed by my ten-millions and millions place.

What year am I? ___ ___ ___ ___

Thousands Hundreds Tens Units

June 6th

June 6th is Nathan Hale's birthday. A hero of the Revolutionary War, he was captured by the British. His last words were, "I regret that I have but one life to lose for my country." To find out the year this hero was born, solve this.

- The two-digit number formed by my tens and units digits is the quotient when 605 is divided by 11.
- My hundreds digit is in the ten-millions place of this number: 234,870,155,961.
- The sum of all of my digits is the missing number: $90 \div \Box = 5$.

What year am I? ___ ___ ___ ___

Thousands Hundreds Tens Units

What Year am I?

June 7th

June 7th is the anniversary of the death of Cochise, the leader of the Apache nation. To learn the year, solve this puzzle.

- My date is a multiple of 2; it is even.
- My hundreds digit is twice the size of my units digit.
- My tens digit is the number of days in one week.
- The sum of all of my digits is 240 ÷ 12.

What year am I? ___ ___ ___ ___
Thousands Hundreds Tens Units

June 8th

June 8th is the birthday of the famous American architect Frank Lloyd Wright. To discover the year he was born, just solve this puzzle.

- The two-digit number formed by my tens and units digits is <u>four more</u> than the product of 9 and 7.
- My hundreds digit is the same as the number of sides in an octagon.
- The sum of all of my digits is the value of one dime, two nickels, and two pennies.

What year am I? ___ ___ ___ ___
Thousands Hundreds Tens Units

What Year am I?

June 9th

June 9th is the birthday of Amadeo Avogadro, the Italian physicist that was the first to recognize the difference between molecules and atoms. He coined the word "molecule." Learn the year he was born; solve this puzzle.

- My hundreds and tens digits are the same digit; their product is 49.
- My units digit is one less than my tens digit.
- The sum of my digits is the perimeter of this figure:

What year am I? ___ ___ ___ ___

                Thousands Hundreds Tens Units

June 10th

On June 10th of this year Judy Garland was born. She was the actress who played Dorothy in the movie *The Wizard of Oz.*. Learn the year she was born by solving this puzzle.

- My tens digit is the same as my units digit; their sum and their product are the same number.
- My hundreds digit is the missing number:
  ☐ x 14 = 126.
- The sum of all of my digits is the number of days in two weeks.

What year am I? ___ ___ ___ ___

                Thousands Hundreds Tens Units

 What Year am I?

June 11th

On June 11th of this year Jeanette Rankin was the first woman to be elected to the House of Representatives. To learn the year, solve this puzzle.

- My date is even and divisible by 5.
- The two-digit number formed by my hundreds and tens digits is the area of this rectangle:

$$\boxed{}\;8$$
$$11$$

- The sum of all of my digits is the difference between 149 and 132.

What year am I? ___ ___ ___ ___

               Thousands Hundreds Tens   Units

June 12th

June 12th is George Bush's birthday. He was the 41st president of the U.S. To find the year he was born, just solve this puzzle.

- The two-digit number formed by my tens and units digits is equal to the product of 12 and 2.
- My hundreds digit is the missing factor of 36:
  1, 2, 3, 4, 6, ____, 12, 18, 36.
- The sum of all of my digits is 64 ÷ 4.

What year am I? ___ ___ ___ ___

               Thousands Hundreds Tens   Units

      86   What Year am I?

June 13th

June 13th is the birthday of Ally Sheedy. She starred in *St. Elmo's Fire*, *Breakfast Club*, and *War Games*. To find the year she was born, solve this puzzle.

- My date is divisible by 2; it's even.
- My units digit is 1/3 the size of my tens digit.
- The two-digit number formed by my hundreds and tens digits is the product of 16 and 6.
- My sum is the average of 30, 11, and 13.

What year am I? _____ _____ _____ _____
       Thousands Hundreds Tens Units

June 14th

June 14th is the birthday of John Bartlett, the editor of *Bartlett's Familiar Quotations*. The current edition has more than 22,000 quotations. To find the year he was born, solve this puzzle.

- My date is an even number and is divisible by 5.
- My hundreds digit is 4 times as big as my tens digit; they are both even numbers.
- The sum of all of my digits is <u>one less</u> than the number of inches in one foot.

What year am I? _____ _____ _____ _____
       Thousands Hundreds Tens Units

            What Year am I?

Arkansas

June 15th

On June 15th of this year Arkansas was admitted as the 25th state of the United States. To learn the year, solve this puzzle.

- The two-digit number formed by my tens and units digits is the product of 9 and 4.
- My hundreds digit is two more than my units digit.
- The sum of my digits is the area of this triangle:

4

9

What year am I? ___ ___ ___ ___

       Thousands Hundreds Tens   Units

Alaska

June 16th

June 16th is the anniversary of the beginning of the Alaskan Gold Rush. Discover the year by solving this puzzle.

- My units digit is the largest single-digit prime number.
- My tens digit is the largest single-digit odd number.
- My hundreds digit is one less than my tens digit.
- My sum is the value of five nickels.

What year am I? ___ ___ ___ ___

       Thousands Hundreds Tens   Units

 What Year am I?

June 17th

June 17th of this year is the birthday of George Cormack, the founder of General Mills. To find the year he was born, solve this puzzle.

- The two-digit number formed by my tens and units digits is the number of years in 7 decades.
- My hundreds digit is the number of sides in an octagon.
- My sum is the average of 13, 20, and 15.

What year am I? ___ ___ ___ ___

Thousands Hundreds Tens Units

June 18th

On June 18th of this year Paul McCartney, one of the Beatles, was born in Liverpool, England. To learn the year he was born, just solve this puzzle.

- My tens digit is five less than my hundreds digits.
- My units digit is 1/2 of my tens digit.
- My hundreds digit is the value of one nickel and four pennies.
- The sum of all of my digits is the product of 8 and 2.

What year am I? ___ ___ ___ ___

Thousands Hundreds Tens Units

June 19th

On June 19th of this year the Statue of Liberty was delivered to Bedloe's Island in New York. To find out the year, solve this puzzle

- My tens and units digits are the same; their product is 25 and their sum is 10.
- My hundreds digit is the number of sides in an octagon.
- The sum of my digits is the missing number:
    $$\square \times 3 = 57$$

What year am I? ___ ___ ___ ___

Thousands Hundreds Tens Units

West Virginia

June 20th

On June 20th of this year West Virginia became the 35th state of the United States. To learn the year, solve this puzzle.

- My units digit, an odd number, is 1/2 of my tens digit.
- My hundreds digit is the same as the number of quarts in two gallons.
- My units digit is the smallest odd prime number
- My sum is the average of 19, 17, and 18.

What year am I? ___ ___ ___ ___

Thousands Hundreds Tens Units

90

June 21st

June 21st is the birthday of Prince William, the son of Pricess Diana and Prince Charles of England. To find the year he was born, solve this puzzle.

- My units digit is the only even prime number.
- My tens digit is four times the size of my units digit.
- My hundreds digit is the number given to the month of September.
- The sum of my digits is the number of nickels in $1.

What year am I? ___ ___ ___ ___

Thousands Hundreds Tens Units

June 22nd

On June 22nd of this year the U.S. Department of Justice was established. To learn the year, solve this puzzle.

- My date is divisible by 10.
- The two-digit number formed by my hundreds and tens digit is the missing number in this problem: $3 \times \square = 261$.
- The sum of all is the perimeter of this rectangle:

What year am I? ___ ___ ___ ___

Thousands Hundreds Tens Units

June 23rd

On June 23rd of this year the first typewriter was patented by Christopher Sholes. To discover the year of this invention, just solve this puzzle.

- My date is even.
- My hundreds and units digits are the same: the largest single digit even number.
- My tens digit is the missing number: $90 \div \square = 15$.
- The sum of all of my digits is one less than the number of inches in 2 feet.

What year am I? ___ ___ ___ ___

Thousands Hundreds Tens Units

 # June 24th

On June 24th of this year there was the first reported sighting of a U.F.O. A man named Kenneth Arnold said he saw the flying saucer over Mt. Rainier, Washington. To find the year, just solve this puzzle.

- My units digit is the number of days in one week.
- My tens digit is the number of quarters in $1.00.
- The two-digit number formed by my thousands and hundreds digits is one less than the number of years in two decades.

What year am I? ___ ___ ___ ___

Thousands Hundreds Tens Units

June 25th

June 25th is the anniversary of the Battle of the Little Big Horn. The leaders of the battle were General Custer and the Sioux chiefs Sitting Bull and Crazy Horse. None of Custer's men survived the battle. To find the of the year of the Battle of Little Big Horn, solve this puzzle.

- My hundreds digit is the number given to the month of August.
- My tens digit is the average of 9, 5, 10, and 4.
- The sum of my digits is the area of this triangle:

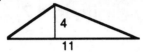

What year am I? __ __ __ __

      Thousands Hundreds Tens   Units

June 26th

On June 26th the bicycle was patented. To find the year this happened, solve this puzzle.

- The two-digit number formed by my tens and units digits is the largest prime number < 20.
- The two-digit number formed by my thousands and hundreds digits is one less than the two-digit number formed by my tens and units digits.
- The sum of my digits is one less than the number of nickels in $1.00.

What year am I? __ __ __ __

      Thousands Hundreds Tens   Units

What Year am I?

June 27th

June 27th is Helen Keller's birthday. She became blind and deaf when she was 19 months old but grew up to become a famous American writer. Solve this puzzle to learn the year she was born.

- The two-digit number formed by my tens and units digits is the number of nickels in $4.00.
- My hundreds digit is the same as the number of sides in an octagon.
- The sum of my digits is 17.

What year am I? ___ ___ ___ ___

Thousands Hundreds Tens Units

June 28th

June 28th is Richard Rodgers's birthday. A famous American composer, he wrote *Oklahoma, South Pacific, Carousel,* and *The King and I.*

- My date is even and divisible by 3.
- My units digit is the only even prime number.
- My hundreds digit is seven more than my units digit.
- The sum of my digits is the missing number: $36 \div 3 = \Box$.

What year am I? ___ ___ ___ ___

Thousands Hundreds Tens Units

What Year am I?

June 29th

June 29th is the birthday of George Washington Goethals, the chief engineer on the building of the Panama Canal. To learn the year he was born, solve this puzzle.

- The two-digit number formed by my thousands and hundreds digits is the perimeter of this figure:

- My tens digit is the number of years in 1/2 a decade.
- My units digit is the same as my hundreds digit.
- The sum of all of my digits is a multiple of 11 and 2.

What year am I? ___ ___ ___ ___

Thousands Hundreds Tens Units

June 30th

On June 30th of this year Niagara Falls was crossed by a tightrope walker named Blondin. To find out the date of this remarkable feat, just solve this puzzle.

- My units digit is the number of sides in a nonagon.
- The two-digit number formed by my hundreds and tens digits is five less than the number of years in nine decades.
- The sum of all of my digits is $92 \div 4 = \square$.

What year am I? ___ ___ ___ ___

Thousands Hundreds Tens Units

         What Year am I?

July 1st

July 1st is the anniversary of the Battle of Gettysburg, fought between the Confederate and Union armies in Pennsylvania. To find the year, just solve this puzzle.

- My units digit is an odd number and is 1/2 of my tens digit.
- My hundreds digit is the missing number in this sequence of numbers: 2,4,6,_____, 10,12.
- The sum of all of my digits is two less than twenty.

What year am I? ___ ___ ___ ___

Thousands Hundreds Tens Units

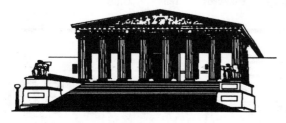

July 2nd

July 2nd is the birthday of Thurgood Marshall. He was the first African American to serve as a Supreme Court justice. To find the year, just solve this puzzle.

- My hundreds digit is the area of this square: ▦ .
- My units digit is the hundreds digit in this number: 4,867.
- The sum of all of my digits is the value of one dime, one nickel, and three pennies.

What year am I? ___ ___ ___ ___

Thousands Hundreds Tens Units

Utah

July 3rd

On July 3rd of this year Utah was admitted to the U.S. as the forty-third state. Solve this puzzle to find the year this happened.

- My date is an even number and is divisible by 5.
- My hundreds digit is equal to 2x2x2.
- My tens digit is one bigger than my hundreds digit.
- The sum of all of my digits is 18.

What year am I? ____ ____ ____ ____
                            Thousands Hundreds Tens Units

July 4th

On July 4th of this year the song *America the Beautiful* was first published. It was written by Catherine Lee Bates. To discover the year, just solve this puzzle.

- My date is an odd number and divisible by 5.
- My tens digit is the missing number in this sequence: 0, 3, 6, ____, 12, 15.
- My hundreds digit is in the ten-thousands place in this number: 329,081,457.
- The sum of all of my digits is half of 46.

What year am I? ____ ____ ____ ____
                            Thousands Hundreds Tens Units

What Year am I?

Venezuela

July 5th

July 5th is celebrated in Venezuela as Independence Day. It is the anniversary of the day the people received their independence from Spain. Solve this puzzle to discover the year.

- My tens and units digits are the same; the first *counting number*.
- My hundreds digit is the largest single-digit, even number.
- The sum of all of my digits is one more than a decade.

What year am I? ＿＿ ＿＿ ＿＿ ＿＿

Thousands   Hundreds   Tens   Units

July 6th

July 6th is the birthday of Helen Beatrix Potter. She was the creator of the Peter Rabbit stories for children. To discover the year she was born, just solve this puzzle.

- The two-digit number formed by my tens and units digits is a multiple of 11 and 6.
- My hundreds digit is the same as the number of pints in four quarts.
- The sum of all of my digits is 21.

What year am I? ＿＿ ＿＿ ＿＿ ＿＿

Thousands   Hundreds   Tens   Units

July 7th

July 7th is Leroy "Satchel" Paige's birthday. He was a great African-American pitcher in the American League. He faced serious racial discrimination when he entered the major leagues. Solve this puzzle to discover the year he was born.

- My units digit is the same as the number of sides in a hexagon.
- My hundreds digit is three more than my units digit.
- The sum of all of my digits is the missing number: 8 x ☐ = 128.

What year am I? ___ ___ ___ ___
Thousands   Hundreds   Tens   Units

July 8th

On July 8th of this year Count Ferdinand von Zeppelin, the German inventor, was born. Can you guess the type of airship he invented? Solve this puzzle to find the year he was born.

- My hundreds and units digits are the same; their sum is 16 and their product is 64.
- My tens digit is the smallest, odd, prime number.
- The sum of all of my digits is the average of 21, 16, 28, and 15.

What year am I? ___ ___ ___ ___
Thousands   Hundreds   Tens   Units

July 9th

July 9th is the birthday of Elias Howe. Born in Brooklyn, New York, he invented the sewing machine. To find the year Howe was born, just solve this problem.

- My thousands and tens digits are the same number.
- My hundreds digit is the missing number in this sequence: 1,___,15,22,29.
- My units digit is one greater than my hundreds digit.
- The sum of all of my digits is 19.

What year am I? ___ ___ ___ ___
Thousands Hundreds Tens Units

July 10th

July 10th is Arthur Ashe's birthday. He was an outstanding African-American tennis player who died, tragically, when he was only 50 years old. To discover the year he was born, solve this puzzle.

- My units digit is the same as the number of sides in a triangle.
- My tens digit is the same as the number of sides in a quadrilateral.
- My hundreds digit is 5 more than my tens digit.
- The sum of my digits is the value of one dime and seven pennies.

What year am I? ___ ___ ___ ___
Thousands Hundreds Tens Units

July 11th

July 11th is known as the "Day of the Five Billion" because the 5 billionth inhabitant of Earth was born. The eight-pound baby boy, named Matej Gaspar, was born in Yugoslavia. To discover the year, solve this puzzle.

- The two-digit number formed by my hundreds and tens digits is two less than 100.
- My units digit is the number of days in one week.
- The sum of all of my digits is 1/4 of a century.

What year am I? __ __ __ __

Thousands Hundreds Tens Units

July 12th

July 12th is Milton Berle's birthday. He was called "Mr. Television" and starred in *The Milton Berle Show*. To find out when he was born, just solve this puzzle.

- My hundreds digit is in the thousands place of this number: 49,807
- My tens digit is one less than my thousands digit.
- My units digit is in the hundreds place of the number above.
- The sum of all of my digits is the quotient when 108 is divided by 6.

What year am I? __ __ __ __

Thousands Hundreds Tens Units

July 13th

July 13th is Mary Wooley's birthday. She was the first woman to graduate from Brown University. She was a teacher and president of a college. To find the year she was born, just solve this puzzle.

- My units digit is an odd number and is 1/2 of my tens digit.
- My hundreds digit is two more than my tens digit.
- The sum of my digits is a multiple of 2 and 9.

What year am I? ___ ___ ___ ___

Thousands Hundreds Tens Units

July 14th

July 14th is a national holiday in France celebrating the fall of the Bastille (a terrible prison) and the start of the French Revolution. To find out the year, just solve this puzzle.

- My hundreds digit is the largest single-digit prime number.
- Add one to my hundreds digit and you have my tens digit.
- Add one to my tens digit and you have my units digit.
- My sum is the area of this square: □⁵

What year am I? ___ ___ ___ ___

Thousands Hundreds Tens Units

July 15th

July 15th is the birthday of Clement Clark Moore. He was the author of "A Visit from Saint Nicholas" ("Twas the Night Before Christmas.") To find out the year Moore was born, solve this puzzle.

- My hundreds and tens digit are the same; their sum is 14 and their product is 49.
- My units digit is in the thousands place of this number: 5,689,012.
- The sum of all of my digits is equal to 120 ÷ 5.

What year am I? __ __ __ __

Thousands Hundreds Tens Units

Richter Scale

July 16th

On July 16th of this year an earthquake measuring 7.7 on the Richter Scale happened in the Philippines. There was enormous damage and terrible loss of life. To find out the year, solve this puzzle.

- My hundreds and tens digits are the sides of this square: Area = 81 square units
- My date is divisible by 10.
- My sum of my digits is 19.

What year am I? __ __ __ __

Thousands Hundreds Tens Units

What Year am I?

July 17th

July 17th is known as Wrong Way Corrigan Day because on this day Douglas Corrigan left Brooklyn, NY headed for Los Angeles, CA. A little over 28 hours later he landed in Dublin, Ireland. He followed the wrong end of the compass. To find the year Wrong Way traveled, solve this puzzle.

- My odd tens digit is 1/3 of my hundreds digit.
- My units digit is the same as the number of sides on an octagon.
- My date is 62 less than 2,000.

What year am I? ___ ___ ___ ___

  Thousands Hundreds Tens Units

July 18th

July 18th is Nelson Mandela's birthday. The son of a tribal chieftain, he was elected president of the country of South Africa. To learn the year he was born, solve this puzzle.

- My units digit is the same as the perimeter of this figure:  .
- My hundreds digit is in the thousands place in this number: 1,249,800.
- My tens digit is in the millions place.
- The sum of all of my digits is the missing number in this problem: ☐ x 4 = 76.

What year am I? ___ ___ ___ ___

  Thousands Hundreds Tens Units

What Year am I?

July 19th

July 19th is the anniversary of the women's conference held at Seneca Falls, New York. It started the Women's Rights movement. Their goal was to get women the right to vote! Solve this puzzle to find the year of this conference.

- My hundred and unit digits are the same; they could be the sides of this square: ■ Area = 64
- My tens digit is 1/2 of my units digit.
- The sum of all of my digits the average of 23 and 19.

What year am I? __ __ __ __

Thousands Hundreds Tens Units

July 20th

July 20th is the birthday of Sir Edmund Hillary, the first man to climb to the summit of Mt. Everest, the highest mountain in the world (29,028 feet). He climbed with his Sherpa guide, Tenzing Norgay. To discover the year, solve this problem.

- The two-digit number formed by my thousands and hundreds digits is the same as the two-digit number formed by my tens and units digits.
- My hundreds digit is the area of the shaded part of

this figure:
- My sum is the same as two decades.

What year am I? __ __ __ __

Thousands Hundreds Tens Units

What Year am I?

July 21st

On July 21st Ernest Hemingway, the great American writer, was born. One of the books he wrote was *The Old Man and the Sea.*. To find out the year he was born, solve this puzzle.

- My tens and units digits are the same; they could be the sides of this square: ▮ Area = 81
- My hundreds digit is one less than my tens digit.
- The sum of all of my digits is equal to 675 – 648.

What year am I? ___ ___ ___ ___
Thousands Hundreds Tens Units

July 22nd

According to German legend, on July 22nd of this year the Pied Piper of Hamelin piped the rats out of town and into the Weser River. To discover the year this is believed to have happened, just solve this puzzle.

- The two-digit number formed by my tens and units digits are the perimeter of this shape: ¹³⬠^{20 16}₂₇ .
- My hundreds digit is 1/2 of my units digit.
- The sum of all of my digits is 17.

What year am I? ___ ___ ___ ___
Thousands Hundreds Tens Units

What Year am I?

July 23rd

On July 23rd of this year Don Drysdale, the Hall of Fame pitcher, was born. He pitched for the Brooklyn and L.A. Dodgers. He had a win-loss record of 209 and 166 and a career E.R.A. of 2.95. To discover the year he was born, just solve this puzzle.

- My tens digit is an odd number but is 1/2 of my even, units digit.
- If you had one nickel and four pennies you would have my hundreds digit.
- The sum of all of my digits is 19.

What year am I? ___ ___ ___ ___

Thousands   Hundreds   Tens   Units

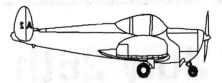

July 24th

July 24th is Amelia Earhart's birthday. She was the first woman aviator to cross the Atlantic solo and to fly solo from Hawaii to California. Find out the year she was born by solving this puzzle.

- My hundreds and units digits are the same; they could be the sides of this square: ▣ Area = 64
- My tens digit is one more than my units digit.
- 52 ÷ 2 equals the sum of all of my digits.

What year am I? ___ ___ ___ ___

Thousands   Hundreds   Tens   Units

107

July 25th

July 25th is Walter Payton's birthday. He was a pro football player and Hall of Famer who played for the Chicago Bears. To discover the year he was born, solve this puzzle.

- The two-digit number formed by my tens and units digits is the area of this rectangle:
- My hundreds digit is the sum of my tens and units digits.
- The sum of my digits is the difference between 1021 and 1002.

What year am I? ___ ___ ___ ___

Thousands   Hundreds   Tens   Units

July 26th

July 26th is the birthday of Mick (Michael Phillip) Jagger, the lead singer of the rock group the Rolling Stones. To find the year he was born, solve this puzzle.

- My hundreds digit is the same as the number of sides on a nonagon.
- My tens digit is the amount of change you would get for $1.00 if you bought something for 96¢.
- My units digit is one less than my tens digit.
- The sum of all of my digits is 17.

What year am I? ___ ___ ___ ___

Thousands   Hundreds   Tens   Units

108

July 27th

On July 27th of this year the armistice agreement that ended the Korean War was signed. To discover the year, solve this puzzle.

- My units digit is the same as the number of sides on a triangle.
- My tens digit is the missing number in this sequence of numbers: 0, _____, 10, 15, 20.
- My hundreds digit is four more than my tens digit.
- The sum of all of my digits is a multiple of 9.

What year am I? ___ ___ ___ ___

Thousands Hundreds Tens Units

July 28th

July 28th is Jacqueline Kennedy Onassis's birthday. The widow of President John F. Kennedy, she later married Greek millionaire Aristotle Socrates Onassis. Solve this puzzle to find the year she was born.

- My hundreds and units digits are the same number: one less than the number of years in a decade.
- My tens digit is the only even prime number.
- The sum of my digits is the number of days in three weeks.

What year am I? ___ ___ ___ ___

Thousands Hundreds Tens Units

What Year am I?

July 29th

July 29th is the sad anniversary of the sinking the American cruiser *Indianapolis* by a torpedo. Of the 1,196 crew members on board, only 318 survived. This was the U.S. Navy's worst loss at sea. To find out the year, solve this problem.

- My hundreds digit is the sum of my tens and units digits.
- My date is an odd number and divisible by 5.
- My tens digit is the same as the number of sides in a rhombus.
- The sum of all of my digits is 19.

What year am I? ___ ___ ___ ___

Thousands   Hundreds   Tens   Units

July 30th

July 30th is the birthday of Henry Ford, the American inventor and namesake of the famous automobile. To find out the year he was born, solve this puzzle.

- My units digit is the missing number in this sequence of numbers: 1, _____, 6, 10, 15, 21.
- My tens digit is twice the size of my units digit.
- My hundreds digit is in the thousands place of this number: 3,798,210.
- The sum of all of my digits is 18.

What year am I? ___ ___ ___ ___

Thousands   Hundreds   Tens   Units

What Year am I?

July 31st

On July 31st of this year the U.S. Patent Office opened and the first patent was issued to Samuel Hopkins. The patent was signed by George Washington and Thomas Jefferson. To find out the year this happened, solve this puzzle.

- My hundreds digit is two less than my tens digit.
- The two-digit number formed by my tens and units digits is the value of nine dimes.
- My sum of all of my digits is the value of one dime, one nickel, and two pennies.

What year am I? $\underline{\hphantom{00}}$ $\underline{\hphantom{00}}$ $\underline{\hphantom{00}}$ $\underline{\hphantom{00}}$

Thousands   Hundreds   Tens   Units

August 1st

August 1st is Herman Melville's birthday. His most famous novel was *Moby Dick.* To find the year he was born, just solve this puzzle.

- The two-digit number formed by my tens and units digits is one more than the two-digit number formed by my thousands and hundreds digits.
- My hundreds digit is the missing number in this sequence of numbers: 2, 4, 6,_____,10, 12.
- The sum of all of my digits is one less than two decades.

What year am I? __ __ __ __

Thousands Hundreds Tens Units

 # August 2nd

On August 2nd of this year the Lincoln-head penny was first issued. To find the year, just solve this puzzle.

- My hundreds digit is the area of this square: ⊞ .
- My units digit is the hundreds digit in this number: 4,267.
- The sum of all of my digits is the same as the value of one dime and two pennies.

What year am I? __ __ __ __

Thousands Hundreds Tens Units

   What Year am I?

August 3rd

On August 3rd of this year Elisha Graves Otis was born. Mr. Otis invented and manufactured the elevator.

- The two-digit number formed by my tens and units digits is the amount of time between 9:12 A.M. and 9:23 A.M.
- My hundreds digit is equal to 2x2x2.
- The sum of all of my digits is one year more than a decade.

What year am I? ___ ___ ___ ___

Thousands Hundreds Tens Units

 # August 4th

August 4th is Louis Armstong's birthday. A famous jazz musician, he played the trumpet. To discover the year he was born, just solve this puzzle.

- The three-digit number formed by my hundreds, tens, and units digits has this word-name:
    nine hundred one.
- The sum of all of my digits is one more than the number of years in a decade.

What year am I? ___ ___ ___ ___

Thousands Hundreds Tens Units

August 5th

August 5th is Neil Armstrong's birthday. The first man to walk on the moon he said, "That's one small step for man, one giant leap for mankind." Solve this puzzle to discover the year of this historical event.

- The two-digit number formed by my tens and units digits is the same as the value of two dimes and two nickels.
- My hundreds digit is the largest single-digit number.
- The sum of all of my digits is seven less than two decades.

What year am I? $\underline{\hspace{1cm}}$ $\underline{\hspace{1cm}}$ $\underline{\hspace{1cm}}$ $\underline{\hspace{1cm}}$

Thousands Hundreds   Tens   Units

August 6th

August 6th is Lucille Ball's birthday. She was famous for her T.V. show *I Love Lucy*. To discover the year she was born, just solve this puzzle.

- The two-digit number formed by my tens and units digits is a factor of 22.
- My hundreds digit is three less than the number of inches in one foot.
- The sum of all of my digits is the same as one dozen.

What year am I? $\underline{\hspace{1cm}}$ $\underline{\hspace{1cm}}$ $\underline{\hspace{1cm}}$ $\underline{\hspace{1cm}}$

Thousands Hundreds   Tens   Units

August 7th

On August 7th of this year, the U.S. satellite, *Explorer VI*, sent back the first picture of Earth from space. Solve this puzzle to discover the year.

- The two-digit number formed by my tens and units digits is the same as the value of 2 quarters, 1 nickel, and 4 pennies.
- My hundreds digit is four more than my tens digit.
- The sum of all of my digits is the missing number:
  $3 \times \square = 72$.

What year am I? ___ ___ ___ ___
Thousands Hundreds Tens Units

August 8th

August 8th is the birthday of Odie, Garfield's sidekick in the comic strip. Solve this puzzle to find the year he was "born."

- The two-digit number formed by my tens and units digits is the amount of change from $1 you would get if you spent 22¢.
- My hundreds digit is two more than my tens digit.
- The sum of all of my digits is the average of 21, 30, 28, and 21.

What year am I? ___ ___ ___ ___
Thousands Hundreds Tens Units

115

August 9th

August 9th is the anniversary of the resignation of President Richard Nixon. He became the first person to resign from the presidency. To learn the year, just solve this problem.

- My tens digit is the largest single-digit prime number.
- My hundreds digit is the missing number in this sequence: 1,___,17, 25, 33.
- My units digit is the number of sides on a rectangle.
- The sum of all of my digits is the number of days in three weeks.

What year am I? ___ ___ ___ ___

Thousands   Hundreds   Tens   Units

Missouri

August 10th

On August 10th of this year Missouri became the 24th state in the United States. To learn the year, solve this puzzle.

- My thousands and units digits are the same.
- My hundreds digit is the product of 2 x 2 x 2.
- My tens digit is 1/4 of my hundreds digit.
- The sum of my digits is the same as one dozen.

What year am I? ___ ___ ___ ___

Thousands   Hundreds   Tens   Units

August 11th

August 11th is Alex Haley's birthday. His famous novel, *Roots*, sold millions of copies and was translated into 37 languages. To find the year he was born, solve this puzzle.

- The two-digit number formed by my tens and units digit is the product of 7 and 3.
- My hundreds digit is two more than the number of days in one week.
- The sum of all of my digits is the missing number:
  $$\square \times 4 = 52.$$

What year am I? ___ ___ ___ ___

Thousands Hundreds Tens Units

August 12th

On August 12th of this year Thomas Alva Edison invented the phonograph. Do you remember records? To find out the year of this invention, just solve this puzzle.

- My hundreds digit is in the hundreds place of this number: 49,807
- My tens and units digits are the same; they could be the sides of this square: ■ Area = 49
- The sum of all of my digits is the quotient when 138 is divided by 6.

What year am I? ___ ___ ___ ___

Thousands Hundreds Tens Units

 # August 13th

August 13th is Alfred Hitchcock's birthday. A movie producer, some of his achievements were *The Birds*, *Psycho*, and the T.V. series *Alfred Hitchcock Presents*. To find the year he was born, just solve this puzzle.

- My tens and units digits are the same; they could be the sides of this square: ▪ Area = 81
- My hundreds digit is the same as the number of sides in an octagon.
- The sum of my digits is the product of 3 and 9.

What year am I? ___ ___ ___ ___

Thousands   Hundreds   Tens   Units

 # August 14th

The man who wrote the famous poem *Casey at the Bat*, Ernest Lawrence Thayer, was born on August 14th. To find out the year, just solve this puzzle.

- My hundreds digit is the largest single-digit even number.
- My units digit is the same as the number of sides in a triangle.
- My tens digit is twice the size of my units digit.
- The sum of all of my digits is the area of this rectangle: ⬚ 9 2

What year am I? ___ ___ ___ ___

Thousands   Hundreds   Tens   Units

What Year am I?

August 15th

August 15th is the birthday of Napoleon Bonaparte. He was emperor of France. To find out the year he was born, solve this puzzle.

- The 'word-name' for the three-digit number formed by my thousands, hundreds, and tens digit is this: one hundred seventy-six.
- My units digit is in the thousands place of this number: 5,689,012.
- The sum of all of my digits is equal to 115 ÷ 5.

What year am I? ___ ___ ___ ___
Thousands Hundreds   Tens   Units

August 16th

On August 16th of this year Menachem Begin, an Israeli hero, was born. As Prime Minister of Israel, he signed the peace treaty between Israel and Egypt. To find out the year he was born, solve this puzzle.

- My hundreds digit is the side of this square:

    Area = 81 square units
- My units digit is 1/3 of my hundreds digit.
- My tens and thousands digits are the same.
- My sum of my digits is the product of 7 and 2.

What year am I? ___ ___ ___ ___
Thousands Hundreds   Tens   Units

 What Year am I?

August 17th

On August 17th Davy Crockett, the American frontiersman, was born in Tennessee. He died at the Alamo. To learn the year he was born, just solve this puzzle.

- My hundreds digit is the largest single-digit prime number.
- My tens digit is the number of sides in an octagon.
- My units digit is the same as the number of sides in a hexagon.
- The sum of my digits is the product of 11 and 2.

What year am I? ___ ___ ___ ___

Thousands Hundreds Tens Units

August 18th

August 18th is the birthday of Virginia Dare, the first child born to European parents in the American colonies. To learn the year she was born, solve this puzzle.

- My tens digit is the same as the perimeter of this figure: ⊞ .
- My hundreds digit is in the thousands place in this number: 1,245,700.
- My units digit is in the hundreds place of this same number.
- The sum of all of my digits is the missing number in this problem: □ x 4 = 84.

What year am I? ___ ___ ___ ___

Thousands Hundreds Tens Units

120

What Year am I?

August 19th

August 19th is Orville Wright's birthday. Solve this puzzle to find the year this first pilot was born.

- My thousands and unit digits are the same; they could be the sides of this square: ▨ Perimeter = 4
- My hundreds digit is the number of pints in 4 quarts.
- My tens digit is one less than my hundreds digit.
- The sum of all my digits is the average of 15 and 19.

What year am I? ___ ___ ___ ___

        Thousands Hundreds Tens Units

August 20th

August 20th is the birthday of Bernardo O'Higgins, the first ruler of Chile after it declared its independence. To discover the year he was born, solve this problem.

- My units digit is the same as the number of sides in an octagon.
- My hundreds and tens digits are the same; they are the area of the shaded part of this shape:

◆◆◆◆◆◆

- The sum of all of my digits is three years more than the number of years in two decades.

What year am I? ___ ___ ___ ___

        Thousands Hundreds Tens Units

Hawaii

August 21st

On August 21st of this year Hawaii became the 50th state of the United States. To find out the year, solve this puzzle.

- My hundreds and units digits are the same; they could be the sides of this square: ■ Area = 81
- My tens digit is the missing number: $75 \div \Box = 15$.
- The sum of all of my digits is equal to $675 - 651$.

What year am I? ___ ___ ___ ___

Thousands   Hundreds   Tens   Units

August 22nd

On August 22nd of this year Ray Bradbury, the famous science-fiction writer, was born at Waukegan, Illinois. His novel *Fahrenheit 451* is about book-burning and censorship. Learn the year he was born; solve this puzzle.

- The two-digit number formed by my tens and units digits is the number of pennies in two dimes.
- My hundreds digit is the missing number:
  $$180 \div 20 = \Box$$
- The sum of all of my digits is a dozen.

What year am I? ___ ___ ___ ___

Thousands   Hundreds   Tens   Units

What Year am I?

August 23rd

On August 23rd of this year Gene Kelly, the actor and dancer, was born. He starred in many movies but two of his most famous were *American in Paris* and *Singin' in the Rain*. To discover the year he was born, just solve this puzzle.

- The two-digit number formed by my tens and units digits is the same as the number of quarts in three gallons.
- If you had one dime, one nickel and four pennies you would have the two-digit number formed by my thousands and hundreds digits.
- The sum of all of my digits is 13.

What year am I? __ __ __ __

Thousands   Hundreds   Tens   Units

August 24th

August 24th is known as Vesuvius Day in Italy because it is the anniversary of the eruption of the active volcano in southern Italy. It destroyed the ancient cities of Pompeii, Stabiae, and Herculaneum. To learn the year, solve this puzzle.

- My tens and units digits is the amount of change you would get from $5 if you spent $4.21.
- The sum of all of my digits is 21 less than 100.

What year am I? <u>A</u> <u>D</u> __ __

Tens   Units

What Year am I?

August 25th

August 25th is Walt Kelly's birthday. He was the cartoonist and creator of the comic strip *Pogo*. Pogo once said, "We has met the enemy and it is us!" To discover the year Kelly was born, solve this puzzle.

- The two-digit number formed by my tens and units digits is the amount of time between 8:50 A.M. and 9:03 A.M.
- My hundreds digit is the number of feet in 3 yards.
- The sum of my digits is the difference between 1018 and 1004.

What year am I? __ __ __ __

Thousands   Hundreds   Tens   Units

August 26th

On August 26th of this year, the first major league baseball game was televised. It was between the Cincinnati Reds and the Brooklyn Dodgers. They played in Ebbets Field in Brooklyn. To find out the year, solve this puzzle.

- My hundreds digit is the same as the number of sides in a nonagon.
- The two-digit number formed by my tens and units digits is the amount of change you would get for $1.00 if you bought something for 61¢.
- The sum of all of my digits is the product of 11 and 2.

What year am I? __ __ __ __

Thousands   Hundreds   Tens   Units

What Year am I?

August 27th

On August 27th of this year Mother Theresa (Agnes Gonxha Bojaxhiu) was born in Yugoslavia. To discover the year, solve this puzzle.

- The two-digit number formed by my tens and units digits is the amount of time between 9:52 A.M. and 10:02 A.M.
- My hundreds digit is one less than a decade.
- The sum of all of my digits is the quotient of 88 and 8.

What year am I? __ __ __ __
Thousands Hundreds Tens Units

August 28th

August 28th is the birthday of Elizabeth Ann Bayley Seton. She was the first American-born saint. Solve this puzzle to find the year she was born.

- My hundreds and tens digits are the same number, the sides of this square: ▦ Perimeter = 28 .
- My units digit is the number of sides in a rhombus.
- The sum of my digits is 19.

What year am I? __ __ __ __
Thousands Hundreds Tens Units

125   What Year am I?

August 29th

August 29th is the birthday of Charlie Parker, the great jazz saxophonist. He worked with other musicians to create the form of jazz known as bop or bebop.

- My date is divisible by 2, 5, and 10.
- My hundreds digit is three less than the number of inches in one foot.
- My tens digit is the only even prime number.
- The sum of all of my digits is a dozen.

What year am I? _____ _____ _____ _____

       Thousands Hundreds   Tens   Units

August 30th

On August 30th of this year, actor Fred McMurray was born in Kankakee, Illinois. He played the father in the T.V. show *My Three Sons*. To find out the year he was born, solve this puzzle.

- My units digit is the missing number in this sequence of numbers: 1, 4, ___, 13, 19.
- My hundreds digit is in the ten-thousands place of this number: 3,098,214.
- My tens digit is in the hundred-thousands place of the same number.
- My sum is the average of 15, 21, 14, and 22.

What year am I? _____ _____ _____ _____

       Thousands Hundreds   Tens   Units

What Year am I?

August 31st

On August 31st of this year Itzhak Perlman, the great violinist, was born in Tel Aviv, Israel. To find out the year, solve this puzzle.

- The two-digit number formed by my tens and units digits is the value of 9 nickels.
- My hundreds digit is equal to the sum of my tens and units digits.
- My sum of all of my digits is the value of one dime, one nickel, and four pennies.

What year am I? $\underline{\hspace{1cm}}$ $\underline{\hspace{1cm}}$ $\underline{\hspace{1cm}}$ $\underline{\hspace{1cm}}$

       Thousands Hundreds Tens Units

September 1st

September 1st is the birthday of Edgar Rice Burroughs. He was the author of the Tarzan books. To learn the year he was born, solve this puzzle.

- My units digit is equal to $25 \div 5$.
- My tens digit is two more than my units digit.
- My hundreds digit is the missing number in this problem: $48 \div \square = 6$.
- The sum of all of my digits is the number of days in three weeks.

What year am I? ___ ___ ___ ___

Thousands Hundreds Tens Units

September 2nd

September 2nd is the anniversary of the Great Fire of London. It lasted three days and burned more than 13,000 homes. There was great loss of life. To discover the year, solve this puzzle.

- My hundreds, tens, and units digits are all the same number.
- If my tens digit were the sides of a square, its area would be 36 and its perimeter would be 24.
- The sum of all of my digits is 19.

What year am I? ___ ___ ___ ___

Thousands Hundreds Tens Units

September 3rd

On September 3rd of this year Labor Day was first celebrated as a legal holiday in the United States. To discover the year, solve this puzzle.

- My hundreds and units digits are both even numbers.
- My hundreds digit is twice the size of my units digit.
- My tens digit is the number assigned to the month September.
- The sum of all of my digits is the average of 18, 24, 13, and 33.

What year am I? ___ ___ ___ ___

Thousands   Hundreds   Tens   Units

September 4th

September 4th is the birthday of Daniel Burnham, a famous city planner. He planned the beautiful lakefront in Chicago and said it should be "forever open, clear, and free." To learn the year Burnham was born, solve this puzzle.

- My hundreds, tens, and units digits are all even numbers.
- My tens digit is 1/2 my hundreds digit.
- My units digit is the same as the number of inches in 1/2 of a foot.
- The sum of all of my digits is 38 ÷ 2.

What year am I? ___ ___ ___ ___

Thousands   Hundreds   Tens   Units

What Year am I?

September 5th

September 5th is the anniversary of the opening of the St. Gotthard Automobile Tunnel in Switzerland. It is the longest car tunnel; it is more than ten miles long and took more than ten years to build. Solve this puzzle to discover the year it opened.

- The two-digit number formed by my tens and units digits is twenty years less than a century.
- My hundreds digit is the largest single-digit number.
- The sum of all of my digits is the number of months in 1 1/2 years.

What year am I? __ __ __ __

Thousands Hundreds Tens Units

September 6th

September 6th is the birthday of Jane Addams. She worked to improve the rights of women and founded Hull House in Chicago to help homeless women. Solve this puzzle to find the year Jane Addams was born.

- The two-digit number formed by my tens and units digits is the missing number: 10, 20, 30, 40, 50, ☐ .
- The two-digit number formed by my thousands and hundreds digits is the quotient you get when you divide 36 by 2.

What year am I? __ __ __ __

Thousands Hundreds Tens Units

What Year am I?

September 7th

September 7th is known as "Grandma Moses Day" to celebrate the birthday of this famous painter. She is called "Grandma" because she did not **start** painting until she was 78 years old. To find out what year she was born, just solve this puzzle.

- My date is divisible by both 5 and 10.
- My tens digit is two less than my hundreds digit; both are even numbers.
- My hundreds digit is the quotient: $96 \div 12 = \square$.
- The sum of all of my digits is equal to 5×3.

What year am I? ___ ___ ___ ___
Thousands Hundreds Tens Units

September 8th

On September 8th of this year the first episode of *Star Trek* was shown on television.

- My tens and units digits could be the sides of this square: ■ Perimeter = 24
- My hundreds digit is three greater than my tens digit.
- The sum of all of my digits is the average of 21, 16, 28, and 23.

What year am I? ___ ___ ___ ___
Thousands Hundreds Tens Units

What Year am I?

September 9th

Colonel Harland David Sanders, the founder of Kentucky Fried Chicken, was born on September 9th. Solve this puzzle to find the year Colonel Sanders was born.

- The two-digit number formed by my tens and units digits is ten less than a century.
- My hundreds digit is the same as the number of sides in an octagon.
- The sum of my digits is the product of 9 and 2.

What year am I? ___ ___ ___ ___

                                 Thousands Hundreds   Tens   Units

---

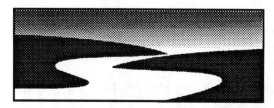

September 10th

On September 10th of this year the first coast-to-coast highway in the U.S. was completed. Solve this problem to find the year.

- My thousands and tens digits are the same.
- My hundreds and units digits are odd numbers.
- My hundreds digit is three times the size of my units digit.
- The sum of all of my digits is the product of 7 and 2.

What year am I? ___ ___ ___ ___

                                 Thousands Hundreds   Tens   Units

What Year am I?

September 11th

On September 11th of this year the first Giant Panda was born in captivity in China. To discover the year, solve this puzzle.

- My odd units digit is 1/2 my even tens digit.
- My tens digit is the same as the number of sides in a hexagon.
- The product of my hundreds and tens digit is 54.
- The sum of all of my digits is the missing number: $114 \div 6 = \square$.

What year am I? ___ ___ ___ ___
                  Thousands Hundreds Tens Units

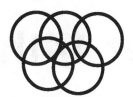

September 12th

September 12th is Jesse Owens's birthday. He won four Olympic gold medals in track and field events. At another track meet at Ann Arbor, Michigan, he broke five world records and tied a sixth in 45 minutes. To find out when he was born, just solve this puzzle.

- The two-digit number formed by my tens and units digits is the quotient when 65 is divided by 5.
- My units digit is 1/3 of my hundreds digit; they're both odd numbers.
- The sum of my digit is the average of 21, 15, and 6.

What year am I? ___ ___ ___ ___
                  Thousands Hundreds Tens Units

What Year am I?

September 13th

September 13th is the birthday of Milton Hershey, the founder of the Hershey Candy Company. To learn the year he was born, just solve this puzzle.

- The two-digit number formed by my tens and units digit is the answer to this problem: 19 x 3.
- My hundreds digit is the same as the number of sides in an octagon.
- The sum of all of my digits is the number of days in three weeks.

What year am I? ___ ___ ___ ___

Thousands Hundreds Tens Units

September 14th

September 14th is the birthday of Constance Baker Motley. She was New York's first Black woman state senator, federal judge, and borough president of Manhattan. She became interested in the law when she was barred from a public beach at age 15. To find out what year she was born, solve this puzzle.

- My thousands and units digits are the same.
- My tens digit is the only even prime number.
- The sum of all of my digits is the difference between 271 and 258.

What year am I? ___ ___ ___ ___

Thousands Hundreds Tens Units

What Year am I?

September 15th

September 15th is Agatha Christie's birthday. She wrote almost 100 books but is most famous for her mysteries. To learn the year she was born, solve this puzzle.

- My date is divisible by 5 and 10.
- My hundreds digit is the next number in this pattern: 0, 4, __, 12, 16.
- My tens digit is one greater than my hundreds digit.
- The sum of all of my digits is equal to 180 ÷ 10.

What year am I? ___ ___ ___ ___

Thousands Hundreds Tens Units

September 16th

September 16th is celebrated as Mexican Independence Day because the Mexican revolution against Spain began on this day. To learn the year, solve this puzzle.

- The two-digit number formed by my tens and units digits is the number of years in a decade.
- My hundreds digit is the number of pints in 4 quarts.
- The sum of my digits is two less than the number of inches in one foot.

What year am I? ___ ___ ___ ___

Thousands Hundreds Tens Units

September 17th

September 17th is Andrew "Rube" Foster's birthday. Called the "Father of Negro Baseball," he was a star pitcher. He won 51 games in one year! To discover the year he was born, solve this puzzle.

- My tens digit is the largest single-digit prime number.
- My units digit is the missing number in this sequence: 1, 4,_____, 16, 25.
- My hundreds digit is the same as the number of sides in an octagon.
- The sum of my digits is the value of one dime and three nickels.

What year am I? ___ ___ ___ ___

Thousands Hundreds Tens Units

September 18th

On September 18th of this year, Harriet Converse became the first white woman to be made an American Indian chief. She was given the name Ga-is-wa-noh, the Watcher, by her adopted tribe. To learn the year, solve this puzzle.

- My thousands and units digits are the same.
- My hundreds digit is one less than my tens digit.
- My tens digit is the number assigned to September.
- The sum of all of my digits is the missing number: $258 - \square = 239$.

What year am I? ___ ___ ___ ___

Thousands Hundreds Tens Units

What Year am I?

September 19th

September 19th is the anniversary of a terrible earthquake that hit Mexico City. It registered 8.1 on the Richter Scale. Nearly 10,000 people died and there was millions of dollars in damage. To learn the year, just solve this puzzle.

- My date is divisible by 5 but not 10.
- The two-digit number formed by my hundreds and tens digit has the value of three quarters, two dimes, and three pennies.
- The sum of my digits is 23.

What year am I? ___ ___ ___ ___

Thousands Hundreds Tens Units

September 20th

September 20th is the birthday of "Jelly Roll" (Ferdinand) Morton. He was a famous American jazz piano player, composer, and singer who was born in New Orleans, Louisiana. To learn the year he was born, just solve this puzzle.

- My odd date is divisible by five.
- The product of my hundreds and tens digits is 64; their sum is 16; and their quotient is 1.
- The sum of all of my digits is the number of pints in 11 quarts.

What year am I? ___ ___ ___ ___

Thousands Hundreds Tens Units

What Year am I?

September 21st

On September 21st of this year hurricane Hugo hit the coast at Charleston, South Carolina. It left billions of dollars in damage in its wake. To learn the year, solve this puzzle.

- Look at the number 860,423. My tens digit is the same as the digit in the hundred-thousands place of this number.
- My hundreds and units digits could be the sides of this square: ▓ Perimeter = 36 .
- The sum of all of my digits is equal to 685 − 658.

What year am I? ___ ___ ___ ___

Thousands Hundreds Tens Units

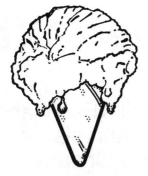

September 22nd

September 22nd is the birthday of the ice-cream cone. Italo Marchiony, the inventor, applied for a patent on this date. Just solve this puzzle to discover the year.

- My units digit is the smallest odd prime number.
- My hundreds digit is three times my units digit.
- My tens digit is the product of 6 x 12 x 9 x 0 x 2.
- My sum is the missing number: 39 ÷ ☐ = 3.

What year am I? ___ ___ ___ ___

Thousands Hundreds Tens Units

138

September 23rd

On September 23rd of this year the planet Neptune was discovered. It is the 8th planet from the sun and is about four times the size of Earth. To find the year it was discovered, solve this puzzle.

- My even tens digit is two less than my even units digit; their product is 24.
- My hundreds digit is twice the size of my tens digit.
- The sum of all of my digits is the quotient of 95 ÷ 5.

What year am I? ___ ___ ___ ___

Thousands Hundreds   Tens   Units

September 24th

September 24th is the birthday of Jim Henson, the man who created the *Muppets* and *Sesame Street*.. Find out the year he was born by solving this puzzle.

- My even units digit is twice the size of my odd tens digit; their sum is 9.
- My hundreds digit is the missing number in this sequence: 0, 3, 6, ____, 12, 15.
- 152 ÷ 8 equals the sum of all of my digits.

What year am I? ___ ___ ___ ___

Thousands Hundreds   Tens   Units

What Year am I?

September 25th

On September 25th of this year the first and only edition of the first American newspaper was published. It was banned because it criticized the British authorities. To discover the year, just solve this puzzle.

- The two-digit number formed by my tens and units digits is the missing number in this sequence:
  50, 60, 70, 80, ____, 100.
- My hundreds digit is the same as the number of sides in a hexagon.
- The sum of my digits is the area of this square: ■4 .

What year am I? ____ ____ ____ ____

Thousands Hundreds Tens Units

September 26th

September 26th is the birthday of the Johnny Appleseed (John Chapman). He planted many apple orchards and was considered a great medicine man by the Indians. To find the year he was born, solve this puzzle.

- My hundreds and tens digits are the same number; they could be the sides of this square: ■ Area = 49 .
- My units digit is the number of quarters in $1.
- The sum of my digits is 19.

What year am I? ____ ____ ____ ____

Thousands Hundreds Tens Units

What Year am I?

September 27th

September 27th is the birthday of Joy Morton, the founder of the Morton Salt Company. To find the year, just solve this puzzle.

- The two-digit number formed by my tens and units digits is the value of one quarter and three dimes.
- My hundreds digit is the same as the number of sides in an octagon.
- The sum of all of my digits is 19.

What year am I? ___ ___ ___ ___

Thousands   Hundreds   Tens   Units

September 28th

On September 28th of this year California was discovered by the Portuguese navigator Juan Rodrigues Cabrillo. To find the year, just solve this puzzle.

- The two-digit number formed by my tens and units digits is the product of 21 and 2.
- My hundreds digit is one more than my tens digit.
- The sum of all of my digits is a dozen.

What year am I? ___ ___ ___ ___

Thousands   Hundreds   Tens   Units

What Year am I?

September 29th

September 29th is the anniversary of the opening of Scotland Yard, London's police headquarters.

- The two-digit number formed by my tens and units digits is the missing number: $2 \times \Box = 58$.
- My hundreds digit is one less than my units digit.
- The sum of my digits is the number of nickels in $1.

What year am I? ___ ___ ___ ___

Thousands Hundreds Tens Units

September 30th

On September 30th of this year Babe Ruth hit his 60th homerun. His record stood for 24 years. To find out the year of Babe's homerun, solve this puzzle.

- The two-digit number formed by my tens and units digits is the number of feet in nine yards.
- Look at: 697,085. My hundreds digit is in the ten-thousands place.
- The sum of my digits is $57 \div 3$.

What year am I? ___ ___ ___ ___

Thousands Hundreds Tens Units

What Year am I?

October 1st

October 1st is the birthday of James Earl Carter (Jimmy), the 39th President of the U.S. He was born in Georgia. To learn the year, just solve this puzzle.

- My units digit is equal to 24 ÷ 6.
- My tens digit is the only even prime number.
- My hundreds digit is the missing number in this problem: 54 ÷ ▢ = 6.
- The sum of all of my digits is two more than 14.

What year am I? _____ _____ _____ _____

Thousands Hundreds Tens Units

October 2nd

On October 2nd of this year the first episode of the *Twilight Zone* was shown on T.V. The show was known for its stories with twist-of-fate endings. To learn the year, solve this puzzle.

- My hundreds and units digits are the same. They could be the sides of this square: ▨ Area = 81 .
- My tens digit is the same as the number of sides in a pentagon.
- The sum of all of my digits is the sum of 18 and 6.

What year am I? _____ _____ _____ _____

Thousands Hundreds Tens Units

October 3rd

October 3rd is Chubby Checker's birthday. He was the rock-and-roll star whose hit record was "The Twist." To learn the year he was born, solve this puzzle.

- My thousands digit is the same as my units digit.
- My hundreds digit is the missing number: $8 \times \square = 72$.
- My tens digit is the same as the number of sides in a quadrilateral.
- My sum is the average of 22 and 8.

What year am I? ___ ___ ___ ___

Thousands Hundreds Tens Units

October 4th

On October 4th of this year the comic strip "Dick Tracy" was first published. To learn the year, just solve this puzzle.

- My units digit is the ten-thousands place in 312,042.
- My tens digit is in the hundred-thousands place of the number above.
- My hundreds digit is three times my tens digit.
- The sum of all of my digits is $56 \div 4$.

What year am I? ___ ___ ___ ___

Thousands Hundreds Tens Units

October 5th

On October 5th of this year Chief Joseph surrendered after taking his tribe on a 1,700 mile retreat. He was chief of the Nez Perce Indians. Solve this puzzle to discover the year.

- The two-digit number formed by my tens and units digits is the product of 11 and 7.
- My hundreds digit is the missing number: ☐ x 9 = 72.
- The sum of all of my digits is 23.

What year am I? __ __ __ __

Thousands Hundreds Tens Units

October 6th

October 6th is the birthday of George Westinghouse. Do you know what his company manufactures? To learn the year Westinghouse was born, solve this puzzle.

- My tens digit is the same as the number of sides in a rectangle.
- My hundreds digit is twice the size of my tens digit.
- My units digit is the number of pints in 3 quarts.
- The sum of my digits is the missing number:
  ☐ x 2 = 38.

What year am I? __ __ __ __

Thousands Hundreds Tens Units

October 7th

On October 7th of this year carbon paper was patented by Ralph Wedgewood. To learn the year this copying method was first used, solve this puzzle.

- Look at this number: 487,601. My tens digit is in the tens place of this number.
- My units digit is in the hundreds place.
- My hundreds digit is in the ten-thousands place.
- The sum of all of my digits is the amount of change you would get from $5 if you spent $4.85.

What year am I? __ __ __ __

Thousands   Hundreds   Tens   Units

October 8th

October 8th is the anniversary of the Great Chicago Fire. Legend says that the fire started when Mrs. O'Leary's cow kicked over the lantern in her barn. Most of the city of Chicago was destroyed by the fire. Find the year of this great fire by solving this puzzle.

- My thousands and units digits are the same.
- My hundreds digit is one greater than my tens digit.
- My hundreds digit is the same as the number of sides in an octagon.
- My sum is the average of 21, 12, 28, and 7.

What year am I? __ __ __ __

Thousands   Hundreds   Tens   Units

     What Year am I?

October 9th

On October 9th of this year, Leif Erikson discovered North America. To discover the year, just solve this puzzle.

- My date is the same as the number of pennies in $10.
- The sum of all of my digits is only 1.

What year am I? _____ _____ _____ _____

       Thousands Hundreds   Tens   Units

October 10th

October 10th is the birthday of the U.S. Naval Academy in Annapolis, Maryland. To learn the year it was founded, just solve this puzzle.

- My whole date is divisible by 5 but not 10.
- My hundreds digit and tens digit are both even numbers.
- My tens digit is the same as the number assigned to the month of April.
- The sum of my hundreds and tens digits is 12; their product is 32.
- The sum of all of my digits is 1/2 of 36.

What year am I? _____ _____ _____ _____

       Thousands Hundreds   Tens   Units

October 11th

October 11th is the birthday of Eleanor Roosevelt. She was the wife of President Franklin Delano Roosevelt; because of her good works, she became known as "First Lady of the World." To find the year she was born, solve this.

- My hundreds and tens digits are the same number: the number of sides in an octagon.
- My units digit is 1/2 of my hundreds digit.
- The sum of all of my digits is the number of days in three weeks.

What year am I? ___ ___ ___ ___

Thousands Hundreds Tens Units

10,000,000

October 12th

On October 12th of this year the first ten-million-dollar U.S. Treasury note was first issued. How tall do you think a stack of ten-million $1 bills would be? To learn the year this Treasury note was issued, solve this puzzle.

- My units digit is the number of days in one week.
- My tens digit is the first odd prime number.
- The two-digit number formed by my thousands and hundreds digits has 1, 2, 3, 6, 9, and itself as factors.

What year am I? ___ ___ ___ ___

Thousands Hundreds Tens Units

October 13th

On October 13th of this year Jesse Lewis Brown was born. He was the first African-American fighter pilot. The ship the *USS Jesse L. Brown* was named in his honor. To learn the year Jesse Brown was born, solve this puzzle.

- My tens digit is the same as the number of pints in one quart.
- My units digit is the same as the number of quarters in $1.50.
- My hundreds digit is three more than my units digit.
- The sum of all of my digits is the missing number:
  $\square \times 4 = 72$.

What year am I? ___ ___ ___ ___
  Thousands Hundreds Tens Units

October 14th

On October 14th of this year Dr. Martin Luther King Jr. was awarded the Nobel Peace Prize. He donated the entire $54,000 to the civil rights movement. To learn the year, solve this puzzle.

- The two-digit number formed by my tens and units digits is the area of this square: ■8 .
- My hundreds digit is the number of dimes in 90¢.
- The sum of all of my digits is the same as the number of years in two decades.

What year am I? ___ ___ ___ ___
  Thousands Hundreds Tens Units

What Year am I?

October 15th

October 15th is Lee Iacocca's birthday. He was the president of Ford Motor Company and later chairman of Chrysler Corporation. To learn the year he was born, solve this puzzle.

- My units digit is the number of sides in a rectangle.
- My tens digit is 1/2 the size of my units digit.
- The two-digit number formed by my thousands and hundreds digit is the missing number: $2 \times \square = 38$.
- My sum is 4 pennies less than 2 dimes.

What year am I? ___ ___ ___ ___

Thousands   Hundreds   Tens   Units

October 16th

October 16th is the birthday of Noah Webster, the "Father of the Dictionary." He was known as a lexicographer. You can look up what this word means one of his dictionaries! To learn the year he was born, solve this puzzle.

- My units digit is the number of quarts in two gallons.
- The tens digit is three less than my units digit.
- My hundreds digit is the same as the number of days in one week.
- The sum of all of my digits is the value of two dimes and one penny.

What year am I? ___ ___ ___ ___

Thousands   Hundreds   Tens   Units

What Year am I?

October 17th

October 17th is known as Black Poetry Day because it is the birthday of Jupiter Hammon. Although Jupiter was born a slave, he was taught to read and was the first African-American to have his poetry published. To learn the year it is thought he was born, solve this puzzle.

- The two-digit number formed by my tens and units digits is the missing number: $132 \div 12 = \square$.
- My hundreds digit is the same as the number of days in one week.
- The sum of my digits is the same as the number of years in one decade.

What year am I? ___ ___ ___ ___

Thousands Hundreds Tens Units

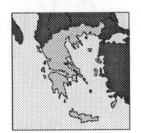

Greece

October 18th

October 18th is the birthday of Melina Mercouri. She was a Greek movie star who was elected to the Greek parliament and was later named Minister of Culture for Greece. To learn the year she was born, solve this puzzle.

- The two-digit number formed by my tens and units digits is the product of 11 and 2.
- My hundreds digit is the number assigned to the month of September.
- The sum of all of my digits is a factor of 2 and 7.

What year am I? ___ ___ ___ ___

Thousands Hundreds Tens Units

October 19th

On October 19th of this year Annie Peck was born. She was the first American woman to climb the Matterhorn in the Swiss Alps. She later climbed the Peruvian peaks, Huascaran (21,812 feet) and Coropuna (21,250 feet). To learn the year Annie was born, solve this puzzle.

- My date is divisible by both 5 and 10.
- My hundreds digit is the same as the average of these numbers: 4, 7, 11, and 10.
- My tens digit is the number of dimes in 50¢.
- The sum of my digits is equal to the number of days in two weeks.

What year am I? ___ ___ ___ ___

Thousands Hundreds Tens Units

October 20th

October 20th is the birthday of Christopher Wren. He was the English architect who designed St. Paul's Cathedral in London. To discover the year he was born, solve this puzzle.

- The two-digit number formed by my tens and units digits is the value of one quarter, one nickel, and two pennies.
- My hundreds digit is two times the size of my tens digit.
- The sum of all of my digits is one dozen.

What year am I? ___ ___ ___ ___

Thousands Hundreds Tens Units

What Year am I?

October 21st

October 21st is the birthday of Dizzy Gillespie, the famous trumpet player. He was one of the founders of modern jazz. Solve this puzzle to learn the year he was born.

- Look at the number 893,715. My hundreds digit is the same as the digit in the ten-thousands place of this number.
- My units digit is the same as the number assigned to the month of July.
- My thousands and tens digits are the same.
- The sum of all of my digits is equal to 675 – 657.

What year am I? ___ ___ ___ ___
Thousands Hundreds Tens Units

October 22nd

On October 22nd of this year President John F. Kennedy ordered a naval blockade of Cuba and forced the Soviets to remove their missiles from the island. To discover the year this happened, just solve this puzzle.

- My units digit is the only even prime number.
- My tens digit is three times the size of my units digit.
- My hundreds digit is the same as the number of sides in a nonagon.
- The sum of all of my digits is 195 – 177.

What year am I? ___ ___ ___ ___
Thousands Hundreds Tens Units

What Year am I?

October 23rd

October 23rd is the birthday of Michael Crichton. He is the creator of the movie, *Jurassic Park* and the T.V. series *E.R.* Solve this puzzle to learn the year Crichton was born.

- My hundreds digit is the same as the number of nickels in 45¢.
- The two-digit number formed by my tens and units digits is the same as the number of days in six weeks.
- The sum of all of my digits is the quotient of 96 ÷ 6.

What year am I? ___ ___ ___ ___

Thousands Hundreds Tens Units

October 24th

October 24th is United Nations Day, a day to celebrate its founding and the adoption of the U.N. Charter. To learn the year it was founded, just solve this puzzle.

- The sum of my tens and units digits is equal to my hundreds digit.
- My units digit is the same as the number of sides in a pentagon.
- My tens digit is the perimeter of this figure: ■ 1
- 57 ÷ 3 equals the sum of all of my digits.

What year am I? ___ ___ ___ ___

Thousands Hundreds Tens Units

What Year am I?

October 25th

October 25th is Pablo Picasso's birthday. He was a famous artist and sculptor. To find the year he was born, solve this puzzle.

- My entire date is a palindrome; it looks the same if you read from left to right or from right to left!
- The two-digit number formed by my hundreds and tens digits is the amount of change you would get from $1 if you spent 12¢.
- The sum of my digits is the product of 2 and 9.

What year am I? ___ ___ ___ ___
Thousands Hundreds Tens Units

October 26th

October 26th is the birthday of Mahalia Jackson, the famous American gospel singer. To find the year she was born, solve this puzzle.

- My tens and units digits are the same number; they are the first counting number.
- My hundreds digit is the amount of change you would get for $1.00 if you bought something for 91¢.
- The sum of my digits is number assigned to the month of December.

What year am I? ___ ___ ___ ___
Thousands Hundreds Tens Units

What Year am I?

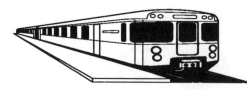

October 27th

October 27th is the anniversary of the opening of the New York City subway. It was the first underground and underwater train in the world. Solve this puzzle to learn the year the subway opened.

- My units digit is the same as the number of quarts in a gallon.
- My hundreds digit is the length of one side of this square: ■ Perimeter = 36 .
- My tens digit is the answer to this problem: 228 x 36 x 0 x 18.
- The sum of all of my digits is the same as the number of days in two weeks.

What year am I? ___ ___ ___ ___

       Thousands Hundreds Tens   Units

Denmark

October 28th

October 28th of this year the first American woman was appointed as an ambassador. She was Helen Eugenie Moore and she served as ambassador to Denmark. Solve this puzzle to learn the year Moore became ambassador.

- The two-digit number formed by my tens and units digits is the same as the area of a square with sides 7 units in length.
- My hundreds digit is the missing number: ☐ x 4 = 36.
- The sum of all of my digits is 23.

What year am I? ___ ___ ___ ___

       Thousands Hundreds Tens   Units

    156   What Year am I?

October 29th

October 29th is the anniversary of the New York stock market crash that led to a decade of economic problems. This time was called the Great Depression. Solve the puzzle and learn the year.

- My tens digit is the same as the number of pints in one quart.
- My hundreds and units digits are the same.
- My hundreds digit is the missing number:
  $72 \div \square = 8$.
- The sum of my digits is 3 less than the number of inches in 2 feet.

What year am I? ___ ___ ___ ___

      Thousands Hundreds Tens Units

October 30th

October 30th is the anniversary of the *War of the Worlds* radio broadcast. People listening thought it was a real news bulletin and panicked when they thought we were being invaded by Martians. Solve the puzzle and learn the year.

- My units digit is the number assigned to the month of August.
- Look at 4,563,089. My tens digit is the thousands place; my hundreds digit is the units place.
- The sum of my digits is $42 \div 2$.

What year am I? ___ ___ ___ ___

      Thousands Hundreds Tens Units

        157   What Year am I?

October 31st

October 31st is the anniversary of the completion of the sculptures on Mount Rushmore. The Presidents whose heads are shown are George Washington, Thomas Jefferson, Abraham Lincoln, and Theodore Roosevelt. The sculptures are 60 feet tall and took 14 years to complete. Solve the puzzle and learn the year.

- My thousands and units digit are the same.
- My tens digit is the number assigned to the month of April.
- My hundreds digit is an odd number.
- The sum of my digits is 45 ÷ 3.

What year am I? ___ ___ ___ ___

Thousands   Hundreds   Tens   Units

November 1st

November 1st each year is celebrated in the Virgin Islands as D. Hamilton Jackson Memorial Day. It is called Victory Day. Solve this puzzle to find out the year this holiday started.

- My units digit is equal to $25 \div 5$.
- My thousands digit and tens digit are the same.
- My hundreds digit is the missing number in this problem: $54 \div \square = 6$.
- The sum of all of my digits is 2 more than 14.

What year am I? ___ ___ ___ ___

Thousands Hundreds   Tens   Units

November 2nd

On November 2nd of this year Daniel Boone was born in Pennsylvania. He was adopted by the Shawnee chief, Chief Blackfish. Daniel's Indian name was "Big Turtle." To find the year he was born, just solve this puzzle.

- The two-digit number formed by my tens and units digits is equal to 17×2.
- My hundreds digit is one-half of 14.
- The sum of all of my digits is 15.

What year am I? ___ ___ ___ ___

Thousands Hundreds   Tens   Units

What Year am I?

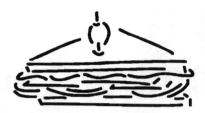

November 3rd

November 3rd is the birthday of the Earl of Sandwich. Can you guess what famous food is named after him? Solve this puzzle to find the year the year the Earl was born.

- My thousands digit is the same as my tens digit.
- My hundreds digit is the missing number:
  $$8 \times \Box = 56.$$
- My units digit is one greater than my hundreds digit.
- The sum of all of my digits is 17.

What year am I? ___ ___ ___ ___

                  Thousands Hundreds Tens Units

November 4th

November 4th is the birthday of Will Rogers, an American humorist. He once said, "My forefathers didn't come over on the *Mayflower*, but they met the boat." What do you think he meant by this? To discover the year Will Rogers was born, just solve this puzzle.

- My units digit is the ten-thousands place in 1,392,042.
- My hundreds digit is equal to my units digit minus 1.
- My tens digit is equal to my hundreds digit minus 1.
- The sum of all of my digits is 100 ÷ 4.

What year am I? ___ ___ ___ ___

                  Thousands Hundreds Tens Units

What Year am I?

November 5th

On November 5th of this year the first crossword puzzle was published in America. Solve this puzzle to discover the year.

- The two-digit number formed by my tens and units digits is the answer to this problem: 144 ÷ 6 =.
- My hundreds digit is the largest single-digit number.
- The sum of all of my digits is 16.

What year am I? __ __ __ __

Thousands   Hundreds   Tens   Units

November 6th

November 6th is the birthday of a famous American musician, John Philip Sousa. He wrote exciting marches, such as *Stars and Stripes Forever.* Solve this puzzle to find the year Sousa was born.

- The two-digit number formed by my tens and units digits is the product of 6 and 9.
- The two-digit number formed by my thousands and hundreds digits is the quotient you get when you divide 36 by 2.

What year am I? __ __ __ __

Thousands   Hundreds   Tens   Units

       What Year am I?

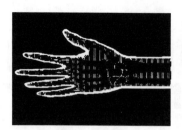

November 7th

November 7th is the birthday of Marie Curie, a famous French scientist. Born in Paris, she worked with her husband, and the two of them discovered the element radium, used in x-rays. To find out what year she was born, just solve this puzzle.

- The sum of my units and tens digits is 13.
- My units digit is one greater than my tens digit.
- My hundreds digit minus 2 equals my tens digit.
- The sum of all of my digits is 22.

What year am I? ___ ___ ___ ___

Thousands Hundreds Tens Units

November 8th

On November 8th of this year Edmund Halley, the scientist, was born. He was the first to sight the famous comet named after him. Halley's Comet will next be seen in the year 2061. Solve this puzzle to find the year Edmund Halley was born.

- My hundreds digit times my units digit equals 36.
- My hundreds digit is one greater than my tens digit.
- My tens digit is the number of sides a pentagon has.
- The sum of all of my digits is the average of 21, 16, 28, and 7.

What year am I? ___ ___ ___ ___

Thousands Hundreds Tens Units

What Year am I?

November 9th

Benjamin Banneker, a well-known African-American inventor and mathematician was born on November 9th. He helped plan the street layout for Washington, D.C. Solve this puzzle to find the year Benjamin Banneker was born.

- My thousands and units digits are the same number.
- My hundreds digit minus 4 is equal to my tens digit.
- The product of my hundreds and tens digits is 21.

What year am I? ___ ___ ___ ___

Thousands Hundreds Tens Units

November 10th

November 10th is the Marine Corps's birthday. At first it was part of the Navy but later became its own branch of the U.S. military. Solve this problem to find the year the Marine Corp was born.

- My whole date is divisible by 5.
- My hundreds and tens digits are the same; their product is 49.
- The sum of all of my digits is 1/4 of 80.

What year am I? ___ ___ ___ ___

Thousands Hundreds Tens Units

What Year am I?

November 11th

On November 11th of this year the song "God Bless America" was first sung. It was written by Irving Berlin. Do you know any other songs written by this composer? To discover the year this song was written, solve this puzzle.

- My units digit is the same as the number of sides in an octagon.
- My tens digit is 1/3 of my hundreds digit.
- The product of my hundreds and tens digits is 27.
- The sum of all of my digits is 21.

What year am I? ___ ___ ___ ___

Thousands Hundreds   Tens   Units

November 12th

On November 12th of this year the French sculptor Auguste Rodin was born at Paris. His most famous piece is called "The Thinker." To find out when he was born, just solve this puzzle.

- My entire date is divisible by 5 and 10.
- My tens digit is 1/2 of my hundreds digit.
- The two-digit number formed by my thousands and hundreds digits has 1, 2, 3, 6, 9, and itself as factors.

What year am I? ___ ___ ___ ___

Thousands Hundreds   Tens   Units

What Year am I?

November 13th

On November 13th of this year Robert Louis Stevenson, the author, was born at Edinburgh, Scotland. Two of the books he wrote were *Treasure Island* and *Kidnapped*. Solve this puzzle to find out the year of Mr. Stevenson was born.

- My tens digit is the same as the number of sides in a pentagon.
- My hundreds digit is the same as the number of sides in an octagon.
- My entire date is divisible by 2, 5, and 10.
- The sum of all of my digits is 14.

What year am I? __ __ __ __

Thousands Hundreds Tens Units

Around the World

November 14th

On November 14th of this year, Nellie Bly set off to travel around the world in less than 80 days. She did! It took her 72 days, 6 hours, 11 minutes, and 14 seconds. To find out what year she traveled, solve this puzzle.

- My hundreds and tens digits are the same; if they were the lengths of the sides of a square the area would be 64.
- The product of my units and tens digits is 72.
- My sum is the difference between 284 and 258.

What year am I? __ __ __ __

Thousands Hundreds Tens Units

What Year am I?

November 15th

On November 15th of this year Zebulon Pike climbed a 14,110 foot mountain. It was later named "Pike's Peak." Do you know what state it is in? To find out when the year the mountain was climbed, solve this puzzle.

- My units digit is the next number in this pattern:

  0, 2, 4, _____.
- My hundreds digit is the next number in the pattern above.
- The sum of all of my digits is equal to 180 ÷ 12.

What year am I? ___ ___ ___ ___

Thousands   Hundreds   Tens   Units

November 16th

November 16th is the birthday of "The Father of the Blues," W.C. Handy. He was born at Florence, Alabama. To find out the year he was born solve this puzzle.

- My hundreds digit is 4 times the size of my units digit.
- The sum of my thousands and tens digits is 8.
- My product of my hundreds and tens digits is 56.

What year am I? ___ ___ ___ ___

Thousands   Hundreds   Tens   Units

What Year am I?

November 17th

On November 17th of this year Elizabeth I became Queen of England. England's current queen is Elizabeth II. To learn the year Elizabeth I became queen, solve this puzzle.

- My hundreds and tens digits are the same; their sum is 10.
- My units digit is the same as the number of sides in an octagon.
- The sum of my digits is a prime number.

What year am I? ___ ___ ___ ___

Thousands Hundreds Tens Units

November 18th

November 18th is Mickey Mouse's birthday. Mickey starred in the first Walt Disney animated movie, *Steamboat Willie*. To learn the year this movie came out, solve this puzzle.

- My units digit is 4 times the size as my tens digit; their difference is 6.
- My hundreds digit is one more than my units digit.
- The sum of all of my digits is divisible by 2, 4, 5, 10, and itself.

What year am I? ___ ___ ___ ___

Thousands Hundreds Tens Units

What Year am I?

November 19th

On November 19th of this year Abraham Lincoln gave the Gettysburg Address. This famous speech contained only 300 words. How long would it take you to read 300 words? Solve this puzzle to find the year of this speech.

- My units digit is 1/2 my tens digit; their sum is 9.
- My hundreds digit is the same as the average of these numbers: 4, 7, 11, and 10.
- The sum of all of my digits is equal to three times my tens digit.

What year am I? ___ ___ ___ ___
Thousands Hundreds Tens Units

November 20th

November 20th is the birthday of the creator of the "Dick Tracy" comic strip, Chester Gould. Some of the crooks Dick Tracey has to deal with are Pruneface, Flattop, Flyface, and Mole. To discover the year Chester Gould was born, solve this problem.

- My date is divisible by both 10 and 100.
- The hundreds digit is a factor of 72.
- The sum of all of my digits is only 10.

What year am I? ___ ___ ___ ___
Thousands Hundreds Tens Units

What Year am I?

PARIS

November 21st

November 21st is the birthday of the French philosopher Voltaire. He once said, "I disapprove of what you say, but I will defend to the death your right to say it.' To find out the year Voltaire was born, solve this puzzle.

- Look at the number 860,423,715. My hundreds digit is the same as the digit in the ten-millions place.
- My units digit is the same as the digit in the hundred-thousands place.
- If you double my units digit and add 1 you get my tens digit.
- The sum of all of my digits is equal to 675 – 655.

What year am I? ___ ___ ___ ___

Thousands Hundreds Tens Units

November 22nd

On November 22nd of this year President John F. Kennedy was killed by a sniper's bullet in Texas. To discover the year this happened, just solve this puzzle.

- My units digit is 1/2 of my tens digit; their sum is 9.
- My hundreds digit is 3 times the size of my units digit.
- The sum of all of my digits is 19.

What year am I? ___ ___ ___ ___

Thousands Hundreds Tens Units

What Year am I?

November 23rd

November 23rd is Harpo Marx' a birthday. Do you know who his famous brothers were? Solve this problem to find the year Harpo was born – you might be surprised.

- My tens digit is three times the size of my units digit.
- The two-digit number formed by my thousands and hundreds digits is a multiple of 2, 3, 6, and 9.
- The sum of all of my digits is the quotient of 126 ÷ 6.

What year am I? __ __ __ __

Thousands Hundreds Tens Units

November 24th

November 24th is the birthday of Scott Joplin, the great American composer and musician. He wrote ragtime music. Do you know what this music sounds like? Find out the year he was born by solving this puzzle.

- My hundreds, tens, and units digit form a palindrome; it is the same right to left as from left to right.
- My hundreds digit is the same as the number of sides in an octagon.
- My tens digit is the perimeter of this figure: ⬛⬛
- 184 ÷ 8 equals the sum of all of my digits.

What year am I? __ __ __ __

Thousands Hundreds Tens Units

What Year am I?

November 25th

November 25th is Joe DiMaggio's birthday. He played centerfield for the New York Yankees. To find the year Joe was born, solve this puzzle.

- The two-digit number formed by my tens and units digits is the area of this rectangle: a rectangle labeled 7 on the bottom and 2 on the side.
- The two-digit number formed by my thousands and hundreds digits is one more than the perimeter of the rectangle.
- The sum of my digits is a factor of 30.

What year am I? ___ ___ ___ ___

Thousands Hundreds Tens Units

November 26th

November 26th is the birthday of the cartoonist Charles Schulz, the creator of "Peanuts." To find the year Schulz was born, solve this puzzle.

- My tens and units digits are the same number; it is the only even prime number.
- My hundreds digit is the amount of change you would get for $1.00 if you bought something for 91¢.
- The sum of my digits is the product of two primes.

What year am I? ___ ___ ___ ___

Thousands Hundreds Tens Units

---

171 What Year am I?

November 27th

On November 27th of this year Anders Celsius was born. He developed the Celsius Centigrade Scale for thermometers. To find the year Celsius was born, solve this puzzle.

- My thousands and units digits are the same.
- My hundreds digit is the 4th prime number.
- My tens digit is the answer to this problem: 17 x 6 x 0 x 8.
- The sum of all of my digits is a multiple of 3.

What year am I? ___ ___ ___ ___

Thousands Hundreds Tens Units

November 28th

November 28th is Paul Shaffer's birthday. Paul is the band leader for David Letterman. Solve this puzzle to find the year he was born.

- The two-digit number formed by my tens and units digits is the same as the area of a square with sides 7 units in length.
- My hundreds digit is the Greatest Common Factor of 18 and 27.
- The sum of all of my digits is 23.

What year am I? ___ ___ ___ ___

Thousands Hundreds Tens Units

What Year am I?

November 29th

November 29th is the birthday of Louisa May Alcott. She wrote the famous book *Little Women*. To find out the year she was born, solve this problem.

- The factors of the two-digit number formed by my tens and units digits are 1, 2, 4, 8, 16, and itself.
- My hundreds digits are the answer to this problem: $112 \div 14 =$

What year am I? ___ ___ ___ ___

Thousands Hundreds Tens Units

November 30th

November 30th is the birthday of Samuel Clemens, better known as Mark Twain. Two of his books are *Tom Sawyer* and *Huckleberry Finn*. Do you know any others? To find out the year he was born, solve this puzzle.

- My date is divisible by 5 but not 10.
- Look at: 1,234,567,089 My tens digit is the ten-millions place; my hundreds digit is the tens place.
- The sum of my digits is $68 \div 4$.

What year am I? ___ ___ ___ ___

Thousands Hundreds Tens Units

         What Year am I?

December 1st

Montgomery, Alabama

December 1st each year is celebrated as "Rosa Park's Day" to honor her role in the civil rights movement. Solve this puzzle to find out the year she was arrested for her courageous actions; then research her role in America's history.

- The two-digit number formed by my tens and units digits is a multiple of both 5 and 11.
- My hundreds digit is the missing number in this sequence of numbers: 3,6, ___, 12,15.
- The sum of all of my digits is 1/5 of 100.

What year am I? ___ ___ ___ ___

                        Thousands Hundreds Tens Units

December 2nd

On December 2nd of this year the first atom was split, bringing in the nuclear age. To find the year of this historic event, just solve this puzzle.

- The two-digit number formed by my tens and units digits is equal to 21 x 2.
- My hundreds digit is one-half of 18.
- The sum of all of my digits is 16.

What year am I? ___ ___ ___ ___

                        Thousands Hundreds Tens Units

What Year am I?

Illinois

December 3rd

On December 3rd of this year Illinois was admitted to the U.S. as the twenty-first state. Solve this puzzle to find the year this happened.

- The two-digit number formed by my thousands and hundreds digit is the same as the two-digit number formed by my tens and units digit.
- My hundreds digit is equal to 2 x 2 x 2.
- The sum of all of my digits is 18.

What year am I? __ __ __ __

          Thousands Hundreds Tens Units

December 4th

On December 4th of this year America celebrated the first Thanksgiving in Plymouth, Massachusetts. To discover the year, just solve this puzzle.

- My thousands and tens digits are the same.
- My hundreds digit is the missing number in this sequence: 0, 3, ____, 9, 12, 15.
- My units digit is in the millionths place in this number: 329,061,457.
- The sum of all of my digits is half of 34.

What year am I? __ __ __ __

          Thousands Hundreds Tens Units

What Year am I?

December 5th

On December 5th of this year Walt Disney was born. Solve this puzzle to discover the year.

- My thousands and units digits are the same.
- My hundreds digit is the largest single-digit number.
- The sum of all of my digits is 11.

What year am I? ____ ____ ____ ____

Thousands Hundreds Tens Units

December 6th

December 6th is Independence Day in Finland. This country gained its freedom from Russia on this date. Solve this puzzle to find the year Finland became independent.

- The two-digit number formed by my tens and units digits is two less than the two-digit number formed by my thousands and hundreds digits.
- My units digit is a factor of 49; my hundreds digit is a factor of 81.
- The sum of all of my digits is 18.

What year am I? ____ ____ ____ ____

Thousands Hundreds Tens Units

What Year am I?

December 7th

On December 7th of this year a book was returned to the University of Cincinnati library after 145 years. The fine due on the book was $22,656. Solve this puzzle to discover the year this happened.

- Both my tens digit and units digit are even. Their sum is 14 and their product is 48.
- My hundreds digit minus 3 equals my tens digit.
- The sum of all of my digits is 24.

What year am I? ___ ___ ___ ___

Thousands Hundreds Tens Units

December 8th

On December 8th of this year George Washington crossed the Delaware with his band of soldiers. Solve this puzzle to find the year this happened.

- My hundreds and tens digits are the same. Their sum is 14 and their product is 49.
- My thousands digit plus my units digit is equal to my tens digit.
- The sum of all of my digits is the average of 21, 16, 28, and 19.

What year am I? ___ ___ ___ ___

Thousands Hundreds Tens Units

December 9th

December 9th is the birthday of Clarence Birdseye. Born in Brooklyn, New York, he found a way to deep-freeze foods and was one of the founders of General Foods Corp. To find the year Birdseye was born, just solve this problem.

- My hundreds and tens digits are the same number; they are the same as the ten-millions place in this number: 387,542,106.
- My units digit is the missing number in this sequence: 1,___,11,16,21.
- The sum of all of my digits is 13 less than 36.

What year am I? ___ ___ ___ ___

                        Thousands Hundreds   Tens   Units

December 10th

On December 10th of this year Ralph Bunche became the first African-American to win the Nobel Peace Prize. He worked to bring peace between Israel and its Arab neighbors. To discover the year, solve this puzzle.

- My whole date is divisible by 5 and 10.
- The difference between my hundreds and tens digits is four.
- The sum of my thousands and hundreds digits is twice the size of my tens digit.

What year am I? ___ ___ ___ ___

                        Thousands Hundreds   Tens   Units

What Year am I?

Indiana

December 11th

On December 11th of this year Indiana was admitted to the United States as the nineteenth state. To discover the year, solve this puzzle.

- My hundreds digit is the same as the number of sides in an octagon.
- My units digit is 3/4 of my hundreds digit.
- The product of my hundreds and units digit is 48.
- The sum of all of my digits is 16.

What year am I? __ __ __ __

Thousands   Hundreds   Tens   Units

December 12th

December 12th is Frank Sinatra's birthday. He was born in Hoboken, New Jersey. To find out when he was born, just solve this puzzle.

- My entire date is divisible by 5 but not 10.
- The two-digit number formed by my thousands and hundreds digits is the average of these four numbers: 21, 30, 12, 13.
- The sum of all of my digits is 16.

What year am I? __ __ __ __

Thousands   Hundreds   Tens   Units

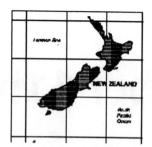

December 13th

On December 13th of this year the island of New Zealand was discovered by Abel Tasman of the Netherlands. Have you ever heard of the Tasmanian Devil? Solve this puzzle to find out the year New Zealand was discovered.

- My units, tens, and hundreds digit is a sequence of even numbers.
- My hundreds digit is three times my units digit; my tens digit is only twice as big as my units digit.
- The sum of my digits is a factor of 26 and 39.

What year am I? ___ ___ ___ ___

Thousands Hundreds   Tens   Units

December 14th

On December 14th of this year the first table tennis (ping-pong) tournament was held. To find out the year, just solve this puzzle.

- My thousands and units digits are the same; they are the first counting number.
- If you add my tens digit to any number, the number will stay the same .
- The sum of all of my digits is the difference between 275 and 264.

What year am I? ___ ___ ___ ___

Thousands Hundreds   Tens   Units

　　　　　　180

December 15th

December 15th is the birthday of Alexandre Gustave Eiffel. He was the French engineer who designed the 1,000 foot high Eiffel Tower. Do you know the city where the Eiffel Tower is located? To find out the year when Eiffel was born, solve this puzzle.

- The two-digit number formed by my tens and units digits is my hundreds digits times 4.
- My hundreds digit is the digit in the ten-thousands place of this number: 5,689,012.
- The sum of all of my digits is equal to $322 \div 23$.

What year am I? __ __ __ __

Thousands   Hundreds   Tens   Units

December 16th

December 16th is the anniversary of the Boston Tea Party. The contents of nearly 350 chests of tea were dumped in Boston Harbor. To find out the year, solve this puzzle.

- My hundreds and tens digits are the sides of this square: ▨ **Area = 49 square units** .
- My units digit is four less than my tens digit.
- My sum of my digits is 18.

What year am I? __ __ __ __

Thousands   Hundreds   Tens   Units

What Year am I?

December 17th

On December 17th of this year the Aztec Calendar Stone was discovered. It weighed nearly 25 tons and was a remarkable calendar. To find the year, solve this puzzle.

- My date is divisible by 2, 5, and 10.
- My hundreds digit is the same as the number of days in one week.
- My tens digit is the number assigned to the month of September.
- The sum of all of my digits is 17.

What year am I? ___ ___ ___ ___

  Thousands Hundreds Tens Units

December 18th

December 18th is Ty Cobb's Birthday. Ty Cobb was a famous baseball player who played in more that 3,000 games. He had a lifetime batting average of .367. To learn the year he was born, solve this puzzle.

- My hundreds digit is the same as the perimeter of this figure: ▭▭▭ ; my tens digit is the same.
- My units digit is in the thousands place in this number: 1,246,800.
- The sum of all of my digits is the missing number in this problem: ☐ x 4 = 92.

What year am I? ___ ___ ___ ___

  Thousands Hundreds Tens Units

   What Year am I?

December 19th

On December 19th of this year the U.S. satellite *Atlas* transmitted the first radio voice broadcast from space. It was a Christmas greeting from President Dwight D. Eisenhower for peace on earth and good will toward people. Solve this puzzle to find the year of this message.

- My thousands digit plus my units digit is equal to my hundreds digit.
- My units digit is the average of these numbers: 6, 10, 8, 7, and 9.
- My tens digit is a factor of both 10 and 15.
- The sum of all of my digits is 23.

What year am I? _____ _____ _____ _____
Thousands Hundreds Tens Units

December 20th

December 20th is known as "Louisiana Purchase Day" to remember when the U.S. purchased more than a million square miles from France for about $20 per square mile. To discover the year of this purchase, solve this problem.

- My units digit is the first odd prime number.
- The hundreds digit is the area of the shaded part of this shape: ◆◆◆◆◆◆◆
- The sum of all of my digits is only 12.

What year am I? _____ _____ _____ _____
Thousands Hundreds Tens Units

What Year am I?

December 21st

On December 21st of this year the Pilgrims landed on Plymouth Rock. To find out the year, solve this puzzle.

- Look at the number 680,423,715. My hundreds digit is the same as the digit in the hundred-millions place of this number.
- My units digit is the same as the digit in the millions place.
- My date is divisible by 2, 5, and 10.
- The sum of all of my digits is equal to 675 – 666.

What year am I? ___ ___ ___ ___

          Thousands Hundreds Tens Units

December 22nd

On December 22nd of this year the first gorilla Colo was born in a zoo. She was born in Columbus, Ohio and weighed only 3 1/4 pounds. To discover the year this happened, just solve this puzzle.

- The two-digit number formed by my tens and units digits are the perimeter of this shape: ⟨7, 13, 16, 20⟩.
- My hundreds digit is 3 more than my units digit.
- The sum of all of my digits is a multiple of 7.

What year am I? ___ ___ ___ ___

          Thousands Hundreds Tens Units

What Year am I?

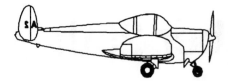

December 23rd

On December 23rd Dick Rutan and Jeana Yeager set a new world record of 216 hours of continuous flight. They traveled 24,986 miles. To learn the year of this flight, just solve this puzzle.

- My tens digit is even but the rest of my digits are odd.
- If you had three quarters, one dime, and two pennies, the number would be the same as the two-digit number formed by my units and tens digits.
- The sum of all of my digits is 25.

What year am I? __ __ __ __

Thousands Hundreds Tens Units

December 24th

December 24th is Kit Carson's birthday. Kit was an American frontiersman and scout who was born in Kentucky. Find out the year he was born by solving this puzzle.

- My units digit minus my thousands digit is equal to my hundreds digit.
- My hundreds digit is the perimeter of this figure:

  ▢▢▢

- 54 ÷ 3 equals the sum of all of my digits.

What year am I? __ __ __ __

Thousands Hundreds Tens Units

What Year am I?

December 25th

December 25th is Clara Barton's birthday. She was a nurse who founded the American Red Cross. To find the year Clara was born, solve this puzzle.

- The two-digit number formed by my tens and units digits is the area of this rectangle: $\boxed{}^{3}$.
  7
- The two-digit number formed by my thousands and hundreds digits is two less than the perimeter of the rectangle.
- The sum of my digits is the difference between 1021 and 1009.

What year am I? ___ ___ ___ ___
Thousands Hundreds Tens Units

 # December 26th

December 26th is the birthday of Steve Allen, a TV star who had the first *Tonight Show*. To find the year he was born, solve this puzzle.

- My thousands and units digits are the same number.
- My hundreds digit is the amount of change you would get for $1.00 if you bought something for 91¢.
- My tens digit is an even prime number.
- The sum of all of my digits is 13.

What year am I? ___ ___ ___ ___
Thousands Hundreds Tens Units

What Year am I?

December 27th

On December 27th of this year Johannes Kepler, one of the world's greatest astronomers and mathematicians, was born in Germany. To find the year Kepler was born, solve this puzzle.

- My hundreds and tens digits are missing numbers in this sequence: 1, 3, ____, ____, 9, 11.
- My thousands and units digits are the same.
- My tens digit is two more than my hundreds digit.
- The sum of all of my digits is a multiple of 7.

What year am I? __ __ __ __

| Thousands | Hundreds | Tens | Units |

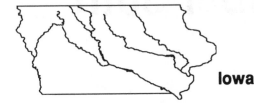

Iowa

December 28th

On December 28th Iowa became the 29th state of the United States. Solve this puzzle to find the year.

- My hundreds digit is twice the size of my tens digit.
- My units digit is 1 1/2 times the size of my tens digit.
- My units, tens, and hundreds digits are all even numbers.
- The two-digit number formed by my thousands and hundreds digits is a multiple of 2, 3, 6, and 9.

What year am I? __ __ __ __

| Thousands | Hundreds | Tens | Units |

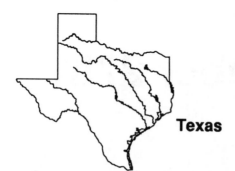

Texas

December 29th

On December 29th Texas became the 28th state of the United States. To find out the year, solve this problem.

- My hundreds digit is twice the size of my tens digit.
- My units digit is equal to my tens digit plus 1.
- My date is divisible by 5 but not ten.
- The sum of all of my digits is 18.

What year am I? ___ ___ ___ ___

Thousands Hundreds   Tens   Units

December 30th

December 30th is the birthday of Bert Parks. He became famous as the emcee of the *Miss America Pageant*. He sang theme song.To learn the year he was born, just solve this puzzle.

- My units digit is the missing number in this sequence: 1, 2, _____, 7, 11, 16.
- My thousands and tens digits are the same.
- My hundreds digit is the in the ten-thousands place of this number: 3,798,210.

What year am I? ___ ___ ___ ___

Thousands Hundreds   Tens   Units

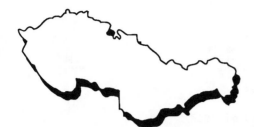

December 31st

At the stroke of midnight on December 31st of this year the state of Czechoslovakia died and the country of Slovakia was born. To find out the year this happened, solve this puzzle.

- My hundreds and tens digits are the same number; they are odd numbers.
- The sum of all of my digits is 21, but my date is divisible by 2.
- My units digit is the only even prime number.

What year am I? ___ ___ ___ ___
Thousands Hundreds Tens Units

January Answers

January 1st:	Betsy Ross created the flag in 1775
January 2nd:	The first junior high school opened in 1910.
January 3rd:	Margarine was patented in 1871.
January 4th:	Louis Braille was born in 1809.
January 5th:	George Washington Carver died in 1943.
January 6th:	It is believed that Joan of Arc was born in 1412.
January 7th:	The first bank opened in 1782.
January 8th:	Bobby Fischer won the U.S. chess championship in 1958.
January 9th:	Blanchard made his hot-air balloon flight in 1793.
January 10th:	Ethan Allen was born in 1738.
January 11th:	Rhubarb was shipped to the U.S. for the first time in 1761.
January 12th:	The first X-ray was produced in 1896.
January 13th:	Stephen Foster died in 1864.
January 14th:	The Pentagon building was completed in 1943.
January 15th:	Martin Luther King, Jr. was born in 1929.
January 16th:	The first national Nothing Day was celebrated in 1973.
January 17th:	Benjamin Franklin was born in 1706.
January 18th:	A.A. Milne was born in 1882.
January 19th:	The tin can was patented in 1825.
January 20th:	The first U.S. basketball game was played in 1892.
January 21st:	Driver's licences were first required in 1937.
January 22nd:	Joseph Wambaugh was born in 1937.
January 23rd:	John Hancock was born in 1737.
January 24th:	Gold was discovered in California in 1848.
January 25th:	Dan Rice was born in 1823.
January 26th:	Michigan became a state in 1837.
January 27th:	Lewis Carroll was born in 1832.
January 28th:	The first telephone switchboard opened in 1878.
January 29th:	The ice-cream cone rolling machine was patented in 1924.
January 30th:	The Lone Ranger was telecast in 1933.
January 31st:	Jackie Robinson was born in 1919.

February Answers

February 1st:	Clark Gable was born in 1901.
February 2nd:	The five stars were named to the Baseball Hall of Fame in 1936.
February 3rd:	The "Day the Music Died" was in 1956.
February 4th:	The Apache Wars stared in 1861.
February 5th:	John Jeffries was born in 1744.
February 6th:	Babe Ruth was born in 1895.
February 7th:	Ballet was introduced to the U.S. in 1827.
February 8th:	The Boy Scouts were "born" in 1910.
February 9th:	William Henry Harrison was born in 1773.
February 10th:	The first singing telegram was delivered in 1933.
February 11th:	Thomas Alva Edison was born in 1847.
February 12th:	Abraham Lincoln was born in 1809.
February 13th:	The first public school was opened in 1635.
February 14th:	Arizona became a state in 1912.
February 15th:	De Aviles was born in 1519.
February 16th:	Edgar Bergen was born in 1903.
February 17th:	Geronimo died in 1909.
February 18th:	The first cow flew in 1930.
February 19th:	Nicolaus Copernicus was born in 1473.
February 20th:	Toothpicks were manufactured in 1872.
February 21st:	Popcorn was first introduced in 1630.
February 22nd:	George Washington was born in 1732.
February 23rd:	The Marines raised the flag on Mt. Surabachi in 1945.
February 24th:	Wilhelm Karl Grimm was born in 1786.
February 25th:	Renoir was born in 1841.
February 26th:	The Grand Canyon National Park was established in 1919.
February 27th:	Longfellow was born in 1807.
February 28th:	The final episode of "M*A*S*H" aired in 1983.
February 29th:	John P. Holland was born in 1844.

190

March Answers

March 1st:	The Peace Corps was formed in 1961.
March 2nd:	Dr. Seuss was born in 1904.
March 3rd:	Alexander Graham Bell was born in 1847.
March 4th:	Casimir Pulaski was born in 1747.
March 5th:	The International Day of the Seal had its birth in 1982.
March 6th:	The Alamo fell in 1836.
March 7th:	The distinguished service medal was introduced in 1918.
March 8th:	The dog license law was passed in 1894.
March 9th:	Amerigo Vespucci was born in 1451.
March 10th:	Paper money was first issued in 1862.
March 11th:	Johnny Appleseed died in 1847.
March 12th:	The Girls Scouts were founded in 1912.
March 13th:	Uranus was discovered in 1781.
March 14th:	Einstein was born in 1879.
March 15th:	Maine became a state in 1820.
March 16th:	*Freedom's Journal* was first published in 1827.
March 17th:	The Campfire Girls were organized in 1912.
March 18th:	The first electric razor was manufactured in 1931.
March 19th:	The swallows first returned in 1776.
March 20th:	The first *Earth Day* was held in 1979.
March 21st:	Juarez was born in 1806.
March 22nd:	William Shatner was born in 1931.
March 23rd:	Patrick Henry gave his famous speech in 1775.
March 24th:	The Exxon Valdez oil spill occurred in 1989.
March 25th:	The production of colored TVs started in 1954.
March 26th:	Justice Sandra Day O'Connor was born in 1930.
March 27th:	This Alaskan earthquake occurred in 1964.
March 28th:	The washing machine was patented in 1797.
March 29th:	Oscar Mayer was born in 1859.
March 30th:	Alaska was purchased in 1867.
March 31st:	Robert von Bunsen was born in 1811.

April Answers

April 1st:	Movies were first censored in 1913.
April 2nd:	The Statue of Liberty was created in 1834.
April 3rd:	Washington Irving was born in 1783.
April 4th:	The Flag Act was passed in 1818.
April 5th:	Booker T. Washington was born in 1856.
April 6th:	Robert Perry reached the North Pole in 1909.
April 7th:	Ravi Shankar was born in 1920.
April 8th:	Hank Aaron set the homerun record in 1974.
April 9th:	Marion Anderson gave her outdoor concert in 1939.
April 10th:	William Booth was born in 1878.
April 11th:	Jane Matilda Bolin was born in 1908.
April 12th:	The big wind occurred in 1934.
April 13th:	The Great Chicago Flood occurred in 1992.
April 14th:	Anne Sullivan was born in 1866.
April 15th:	Leonardo da Vinci was born in 1452.
April 16th:	Wilbur Wright was born in 1867.
April 17th:	Fire escapes first appeared on apartment buildings in 1860.
April 18th:	The Great San Francisco Earthquake occurred in 1906.
April 19th:	The Revolutionary War started in 1775.
April 20th:	Daniel French was born in 1850.
April 21st:	Friedrich Froebel was born in 1782.
April 22nd:	Babe Ruth made his pitching debut in 1914.
April 23rd:	William Shakespeare was born in 1564.
April 24th:	The Library of Congress was started in 1800.
April 25th:	The first seeing eye-dog was presented in 1923.
April 26th:	Charles Richter was born in 1900.
April 27th:	Walter Lantz was born in 1900.
April 28th:	Jay Leno was born in 1950.
April 29th:	Duke Ellington was born in 1899.
April 30th:	Louisiana became a state in 1812.

May Answers

May 1st:	The Empire State Building was dedicated in 1931.
May 2nd:	Catherine the Great was born in 1729.
May 3rd:	Golda Meir was born in 1898.
May 4th:	Audrey Hepburn was born in 1929.
May 5th:	The Battle of Puebla was in 1862.
May 6th:	The Hindenburg exploded in 1937.
May 7th:	Brahms was born in 1833.
May 8th:	DeSoto discovered the Mississippi in 1541.
May 9th:	The first newspaper cartoon was published in 1754.
May 10th:	The Chicago Planetarium was opened in 1930.
May 11th:	Minnesota became a state in 1858.
May 12th:	Florence Nightingale was born in 1820.
May 13th:	Jamestown was founded in 1607.
May 14th:	Fahrenheit was born in 1686.
May 15th:	Frank Baum was born in 1905.
May 16th:	The 5¢ piece was minted in 1866.
May 17th:	The New York Stock Exchange started in 1792.
May 18th:	Pope John Paul II was born in 1920.
May 19th:	Malcolm X was born in 1925.
May 20th:	Dolly Madison was born in 1768.
May 21st:	The Red Cross was founded in 1881.
May 22nd:	Sir Arthur Conan Doyle was born in 1859.
May 23rd:	Sgt. William Carney received his medal in 1900.
May 24th:	The Brooklyn Bridge opened in 1883.
May 25th:	Bill "Bojangles" Robinson was born in 1878.
May 26th:	Dr. Sally Kirsten Ride was born in 1951.
May 27th:	Rachel Carson was born in 1907.
May 28th:	The Dionne quintuplets were born in 1934.
May 29th:	Wisconsin became a state in 1848.
May 30th:	The first daily newspaper was first published in 1783.
May 31st:	Clint Eastwood was born in 1930.

June Answers

June 1st:	Kentucky became a state in 1792.
June 2nd:	American Indians became citizens in 1924.
June 3rd:	Jefferson Davis was born in 1808.
June 4th:	King George III was born in 1738.
June 5th:	The first balloon flight occurred in 1783.
June 6th:	Nathan Hale was born in 1755.
June 7th:	Cochise died in 1874.
June 8th:	Frank Lloyd Wright was born in 1867.
June 9th:	Amadeo Avogadro was born in 1776.
June 10th:	Judy Garland was born in 1922.
June 11th:	Jeanette Rankin was born in 1880.
June 12th:	George Bush was born in 1924.
June 13th:	Ally Sheedy was born in 1962.
June 14th:	John Bartlett was born in 1820.
June 15th:	Arkansas became a state in 1836.
June 16th:	The Alaskan Gold Rush began in 1897.
June 17th:	George Cormack was born in 1870.
June 18th:	Paul McCartney was born in 1942.
June 19th:	The Statue of Liberty was delivered in 1855.
June 20th:	West Virginia became a state in 1863.
June 21st:	Prince William was born in 1982.
June 22nd:	The Department of Justice was established in 1870.
June 23rd:	The typewriter was patented in 1868.
June 24th:	The UFO sighting occurred in 1947.
June 25th:	The Battle of Little Big Horn occurred in 1876.
June 26th:	The bicycle was patented in 1819.
June 27th:	Helen Keller was born in 1880.
June 28th:	Richard Rodgers was born in 1902.
June 29th:	George Washington Goethals was born in 1858.
June 30th:	Blodin walked the tightrope in 1859.

July Answers

July 1st:	The Battle of Gettysburg was fought in 1863.
July 2nd:	Thurgood Marshall was born in 1908.
July 3rd:	Idaho became a state in 1890.
July 4th:	*America the Beautiful* was published in 1895.
July 5th:	Venezuela became independent in 1811.
July 6th:	Helen Beatrix Potter was born in 1866.
July 7th:	Leroy "Satchel" Paige was born in 1906.
July 8th:	Count Ferdinand von Zeppelin was born in 1838.
July 9th:	Elias Howe was born in 1819.
July 10th:	Arthur Ashe was born in 1943.
July 11th:	The five-billionth child was born in 1987.
July 12th:	Milton Berle was born in 1908.
July 13th:	Mary Woolley was born in 1863.
July 14th:	The Bastille fell in 1789.
July 15th:	Clement Clark Moore was born in 1779.
July 16th:	The powerful earthquake occurred in 1990.
July 17th:	"Wrong Way Corrigan's" journal occurred in 1938.
July 18th:	Nelson Mandela was born in 1918.
July 19th:	The Woman's Conference occurred in 1848.
July 20th:	Sir Edmund Hillary was born in 1919.
July 21st:	Ernest Hemingway was born in 1899.
July 22nd:	The Pied Piper piped in 1376.
July 23rd:	Don Drysdale was born in 1936.
July 24th:	Amelia Earhart was born in 1898.
July 25th:	Walter Payton was born in 1954.
July 26th:	Mick Jagger was born in 1943.
July 27th:	The Korean armistice was signed in 1953.
July 28th:	Jacqueline Kennedy Onassis was born in 1929.
July 29th:	The *Indianapolis* was sunk in 1945.
July 30th:	Henry Ford was born in 1863.
July 31st:	The U.S. Patent Office opened in 1790.

August Answers

August 1st:	Melville was born in 1819.
August 2nd:	The Lincoln penny was first issued in 1902.
August 3rd:	Otis was born in 1811.
August 4th:	Louis Armstrong was born in 1901.
August 5th:	Neil Armstrong was born in 1930.
August 6th:	Lucille Ball was born in 1911.
August 7th:	The first picture from space came back in 1959.
August 8th:	Odie appeared in the comic strip in 1978.
August 9th:	Richard Nixon resigned in 1974.
August 10th:	Missouri became a state in 1821.
August 11th:	Alex Haley was born in 1921.
August 12th:	The phonograph was invented in 1877.
August 13th:	Alfred Hitchcock was born in 1899.
August 14th:	Ernest Thayer was born in 1863.
August 15th:	Napoleon was born in 1769.
August 16th:	Menachem Begin was born in 1913.
August 17th:	Davy Crockett was born in 1786.
August 18th:	Virginia Dare was born in 1587.
August 19th:	Orville Wright was born in 1871.
August 20th:	Bernardo O'Higgins was born in 1778.
August 21st:	Hawaii became a state in 1959.
August 22nd:	Ray Bradbury was born in 1920.
August 23rd:	Gene Kelly was born in 1912.
August 24th:	Vesuvius erupted in A.D. 79.
August 25th:	Walt Kelly was born in 1913.
August 26th:	Baseball was first televised in 1939.
August 27th:	Mother Theresa was born in 1910.
August 28th:	Elizabeth Ann Bayley Seton was born in 1774.
August 29th:	Charlie Parker was born in 1920.
August 30th:	Fred McMurray was born in 1908.
August 31st:	Itzhak Perlman was born in 1945.

 What Year am I?

September Answers

September 1st:	Edgar Rice Burroughs was born in 1875.
September 2nd:	London had its great fire in 1666.
September 3rd:	Labor Day was first celebrated in 1894.
September 4th:	Daniel Burnham was born in 1846.
September 5th:	The St. Gotthard Tunnel was opened in 1980.
September 6th:	Jane Addams was born in 1860.
September 7th:	Grandma Moses was born in 1860.
September 8th:	*Star Trek* first aired in 1966.
September 9th:	Colonel Sanders was born in 1890.
September 10th:	The first U.S. coast-to-coast highway was completed in 1913.
September 11th:	The first Giant Panda was born in captivity in 1963.
September 12th:	Jesse Owens was born in 1913.
September 13th:	Milton Hershey was born in 1857.
September 14th:	Constance Motley was born in 1921.
September 15th:	Agatha Christie was born in 1890.
September 16th:	The Mexican Revolution began in 1810.
September 17th:	Rube Foster was born in 1879.
September 18th:	Harriet Converse became an Indian Chief in 1891.
September 19th:	The Mexico City earthquake occured in 1985.
September 20th:	Jelly Roll Morton was born in 1885.
September 21st:	Hurricane Hugo hit the east coast in 1989.
September 22nd:	The ice cream cone was "born" in 1903.
September 23rd:	Planet Neptune was first seen in 1846.
September 24th:	Jim Henson was born in 1936.
September 25th:	The first newspaper was published in 1690.
September 26th:	Johnny Appleseed was born in 1774.
September 27th:	Joy Morton was born in 1855.
September 28th:	California was discovered in 1542.
September 29th:	Scotland Yard opened in 1829.
September 30th:	Babe Ruth hit his 60th homerun in 1927.

October Answers

October 1st:	Jimmy Carter was born in 1924.
October 2nd:	*Twilight Zone* first aired in 1959.
October 3rd:	Chubby Checker was born in 1941.
October 4th:	"Dick Tracy" was first published in 1931.
October 5th:	Chief Joseph surrendered in 1877.
October 6th:	George Westinghouse was born in 1846.
October 7th:	Carbon paper was patented in 1806.
October 8th:	The Chicago Fire occurred in 1871.
October 9th:	Leif Erikson discovered North America in 1000.
October 10th:	The U.S. Naval Academy opened in 1845.
October 11th:	Eleanor Roosevelt was born in 1884.
October 12th:	The ten-million-dollar note was issued in 1837.
October 13th:	Jesse Lewis Brown was born in 1926.
October 14th:	Dr. King received the Nobel Peace Prize in 1964.
October 15th:	Lee Iacocca was born in 1924.
October 16th:	Noah Webster was born in 1758.
October 17th:	Jupiter Hammon was born in 1711.
October 18th:	Melina Mercouri was born in 1922.
October 19th:	Annie Peck was born in 1850.
October 20th:	Christopher Wren was born in 1632.
October 21st:	Dizzy Gillespie was born in 1917.
October 22nd:	President Kennedy blockaded Cuba in 1962.
October 23rd:	Michael Crichton was born in 1942.
October 24th:	The United Nations adopted its Charter in 1945.
October 25th:	Picasso was born in 1881.
October 26th:	Mahalia Jackson was born in 1911.
October 27th:	The New York City subway opened in 1904.
October 28th:	Helen Eugenie Moore became Ambassador to Denmark in 1949.
October 29th:	The Stock Market Crash occurred in 1929.
October 30th:	The *War of the Worlds* broadcast was heard in 1938.
October 31st:	Mount Rushmore was completed in 1941.

November Answers

November 1st:	Liberty Day in the Virgin Islands was established in 1915.
November 2nd:	Daniel Boone was born in 1734.
November 3rd:	The Earl of Sandwich was born in 1718.
November 4th:	Will Rogers was born in 1879 in (what is now) Oklahoma.
November 5th:	The crossword puzzle was published in 1924.
November 6th:	Sousa was born in 1854.
November 7th:	Marie Curie was born in 1867.
November 8th:	Edmund Halley was born in 1656.
November 9th:	Benjamin Banneker was born in 1731.
November 10th:	The Marine Corps was born in 1775.
November 11th:	*God Bless America* was first performed in 1938.
November 12th:	Rodin was born in 1840.
November 13th:	Robert Louis Stevenson was born in 1850.
November 14th:	Nellie Bly set off on her journey in 1889.
November 15th:	Pike climbed the mountain in 1806.
November 16th:	W.C. Handy was born in 1872.
November 17th:	Elizabeth I was became queen in 1558.
November 18th:	Mickey Mouse was born in 1928.
November 19th:	Lincoln gave the Gettysburg Adress in 1863.
November 20th:	Chester Gould was born in 1900.
November 21st:	Voltaire was born in 1694.
November 22nd:	John F. Kennedy was assassinated in 1963.
November 23rd:	Harpo Marx was born in 1893.
November 24th:	Scott Joplin was born in 1868.
November 25th:	Joe DiMaggio was born in 1914.
November 26th:	Charles Schulz was born in 1922.
November 27th:	Anders Celsius was born in 1701.
November 28th:	Paul Shaffer was born in 1949.
November 29th:	Louisa May Alcott was born in 1832.
November 30th:	Samuel Clemens was born in 1835.

December Answers

December 1st:	Rosa Parks was arrested in 1955.
December 2nd:	The atom was split in 1942.
December 3rd:	Illinois became a state in 1818.
December 4th:	The first Thanksgiving was celebrated in 1619.
December 5th:	Walt Disney was born in 1901.
December 6th:	Finland gained its independence in 1917.
December 7th:	The book was returned in 1968.
December 8th:	Washington crossed the Delaware in 1776.
December 9th:	Clarence Birdseye was born in 1886.
December 10th:	Ralph Bunche won the Nobel Peace Prize in 1950.
December 11th:	Indiana was admitted to the U.S. in 1816.
December 12th:	Frank Sinatra was born in 1915.
December 13th:	New Zealand was discovered in 1642.
December 14th:	The first table tennis tournament was held in 1901.
December 15th:	Eiffel was born in 1832.
December 16th:	The Boston Tea Party occurred in 1773.
December 17th:	The Aztec Calendar Stone was discovered in 1790.
December 18th:	Ty Cobb was born in 1886.
December 19th:	The message was sent from space in 1958.
December 20th:	Louisiana Purchase occurred in 1803.
December 21st:	Pilgrims landed in 1620.
December 22nd:	Colo was born in 1956.
December 23rd:	The continuous airplane flight was in 1987.
December 24th:	Kit Carson was born in 1809.
December 25th:	Clara Barton was born in 1821.
December 26th:	Steve Allen was born in 1921.
December 27th:	Johannes Kepler was born in 1571.
December 28th:	Iowa became a state in 1846.
December 29th:	Texas became a state in 1845.
December 30th:	Bert Parks was born in 1914.
December 31st:	Slovakia was born in 1992.